with

Coping

ANXIETY AND PANIC ATTACKS

Jordan Lee

The Rosen Publishing Group, Inc.
New York

Published in 1997, 2000 by The Rosen Publishing Group, Inc.
29 East 21st Street, New York, NY 10010

Copyright © 1997, 2000 by Jordan Lee

Revised Edition

Cover photo by Olga Vega

Library of Congress Cataloging-in-Publication Data

Lee, Jordan.
Coping with anxiety and panic attacks / Jordan Lee.
p. cm. – (Coping)
Includes bibliographical references and index.
ISBN 0–8239–3202–8 (lib. bdg.)
1. Anxiety. 2. Anxiety in adolescence. 1. Title. II. Series.
2. RC531L345 1997
616.85'223—dc2l
                                        97–14367
                                          CIP
                                          AC

Manufactured in the United States of America

About the Author

Jordan Lee has been a psychotherapist since 1976. She currently practices in Tulsa, Oklahoma, where she also teaches psychology at Tulsa Community College. She is a coordinator for Anxiety Screening Day in Tulsa.

Acknowledgments

Many thanks to Dwain Simpson for identifying useful Web sites for me, and to Jaime Simpson for her help in collecting data for this revised edition.

Contents

Introduction

One afternoon as I was walking home from high school, I realized that I was being followed. A car had been slowly moving along behind me, and when I'd look around, the driver would speed up and pass me, only to slow down again. As I neared my neighborhood, I decided to take a shortcut. But as I scurried down a side street, I saw the car parked at the end of the street. Panic seized me. Someone was waiting for me at the end of the street. My heart started pounding, my insides turned to ice, and I turned around and ran for the nearest convenience store. I've never run so fast.

In this case, panic served me well. Faced with certain danger, my body reacted with the age-old fight or flight response, enabling me to escape. My heart sped up; blood was diverted to my legs so I could run faster, and I breathed harder to get more oxygen. The panic reaction when faced with danger is a normal, adaptive reaction. It puts you in a better position to flee danger or turn to fight it.

Sometimes, however, symptoms of anxiety or panic occur when there is no visible threat. Some people feel just the way I felt when that man was following me, except that they are merely walking into a grocery store.

Clearly, something is wrong when anxiety and panic kick in and no danger is present. It is no longer adaptive or normal. I wrote this book because I, like 19 million Americans, suffer from anxiety, and I've learned to manage it. You can, too. Some of you may be very shy teenagers who panic when you're around a lot of people. Believe it or not, that's a very common social phobia that most adolescents outgrow.

There are many different types and symptoms of anxiety disorders. For some of you, there may be thoughts or actions—like saying certain phrases or washing your hands—that you feel as though you must repeat over and over to quell anxiety. Those, too, are signs of an anxiety disorder—obsessive-compulsive disorder. Obsessive-compulsive disorder, or OCD, frequently begins in the teenage years, although it's often not diagnosed until later.

Phobias—or extreme fears of specific things, like heights, spiders, or thunderstorms—can happen to teenagers and even young kids. Sometimes the fear springs from a traumatic experience; sometimes it's not related to anything at all.

This book discusses the six major anxiety disorders, exploring what may cause them and how to treat them. It looks at ordinary stress and discusses ways to avoid going from "stressed" to "anxious and panicked." If you can learn better ways to manage stress, you can overcome many of your fears and go on to lead a happier and more productive life.

Part I:
The Six Types of Anxiety Disorders

Generalized Anxiety Disorder, Panic Attacks, and Post-Traumatic Stress Disorder

Over 19 million Americans suffer from some type of anxiety disorder. This chapter discusses three of them: generalized anxiety disorder (GAD), in which the person experiences extreme chronic anxiety; panic attacks, where symptoms mimic a heart attack and cause the person to believe that he or she is dying; and post-traumatic stress disorder (PTSD), a condition that can include panic attacks and flashbacks brought about by a traumatic event. In all of these disorders, the symptoms of anxiety prevent the person from handling the day-to-day tasks of ordinary life.

Generalized Anxiety Disorder

Chronic anxiety involves three main reactions: physiological (the physical sensations), cognitive (the ways people think about their situation), and behavioral (what people do about their situation).

The most common physiological sensations of generalized anxiety are gastrointestinal upsets: butterflies in the stomach, nausea, vomiting, and diarrhea. To relieve these symptoms, you may take antacids or antidiarrheal medication, especially when you face an anxiety-provoking event. Many people with these reactions end up with ulcers. Other common complaints include frequent headaches and bruxism (clenching or grinding of the teeth).

Cognitive reactions to stress—the way you think about anxiety—may make it worse. For instance, if someone is constantly worrying about getting sick to his stomach, he may actually help bring on the sickness. A person may also become very sensitive emotionally, feeling criticized, edgy, irritable, or jittery.

Our behavior can also worsen the symptoms of anxiety. Avoiding certain situations will reinforce the fears already associated with that situation. Why? When we run away from a fearful situation, we feel relief. But each time we avoid the stressful event, we are actually strengthening our belief that we are unable to deal successfully with the situation. The temporary reduction of anxiety may feel good, but ultimately it will make overcoming the anxiety far more difficult.

While reading this book, you may start thinking that these symptoms and reactions sound familiar. Just remember: Only a trained professional, such as a psychologist, social worker, outpatient therapist, psychiatrist, or clinical nurse, can make a proper diagnosis of an anxiety disorder.

Panic Attacks with and Without Agoraphobia

Panic is the body's way of preparing a person to flee or fight when encountering a threat. Because panic attacks are so disabling to some, they may lead to agoraphobia—

a fear of leaving the house. More than 2.4 million Americans suffer from panic attacks.

Fear or panic are normal reactions to danger. They set off a chain of events in the body by activating the autonomic nervous system, which controls our breathing, digestion, and temperature regulation. The autonomic nervous system is composed of two parts: the sympathetic nervous system (SNS) and the parasympathetic nervous system (PNS). The job of the SNS is to rev a person up, whereas the job of the PNS is to calm that person down. The two parts balance each other out.

When you're frightened, the SNS releases adrenaline with dramatic results. Your heart pumps harder to make your blood circulate more quickly through your body to where it's most needed. You're aware only of your pounding, racing heart or the tingling sensations in your hands and feet. That's because blood is being diverted from the hands and feet to the larger muscles.

Your lungs get into the action, too. They work harder to draw in more air. You start to breathe harder and faster, and to sweat. The adrenaline causes you to focus more intently on the immediate danger. Your body is now totally aroused and ready to fight.

Were it not for the PNS, your body would remain aroused indefinitely, and the heightened responses would wreak havoc with your health. Thus, once the danger is past, the PNS takes over, destroying the adrenaline and bringing the body back into a relaxed state.

A panic attack occurs when the body has these heightened responses and no danger is present. Your SNS is activated, but since there is no danger to contend with, the body can't get rid of the adrenaline. Eventually, the PNS kicks in and the symptoms diminish. In the meantime, you may be left wondering if you're about to die. Since you see no visible danger, you may decide the danger is inside yourself. You may think you're having a heart attack.

Many anxious people run to the nearest emergency room only to learn that their EKG reveals no sign of heart trouble. They're told they've had a panic attack. In an attempt to make sense out of the panic, they look for a possible cause. Once they think they've located that cause, they avoid it in the future. This avoidance may eventually lead to agoraphobia.

Agoraphobia literally means a fear of the marketplace, and people often assume that this means a fear of open places. Yet agoraphobics fear more than just open areas. Above all else, agoraphobics are afraid they will suffer a panic attack in public and not be able to get back to safety. As a result, they fear malls, other people's houses, church, concert halls, school, and sports arenas—just about every place except the safety of their own home.

For example, LaDawn Harris's mother suffered from panic attacks with agoraphobia. She rarely left the house unless she took an extra dose of her medication. Even then, she would not mingle with other people.

LaDawn once invited her mother to her soccer game. When Mrs. Harris saw that she was hemmed in on all sides by people, she panicked. She felt her heart racing and she couldn't get enough air into her lungs. The harder she breathed, the more dizzy she became. Her fingers felt tingly, and she thought, "I'm going to faint. I'm going to faint right here in front of everyone."

Sweat poured down her face. LaDawn was on the field; there was no one to help her.

Mrs. Harris suddenly stood up. "I've got to get out of here!" she screamed. She pushed some teenagers aside and worked her way to the side of the bleachers. "Let me by," she kept saying. Other parents were looking at her and whispering. She didn't care. She needed to get back to her car where she could breathe.

She ran the length of the field to the parking lot, searching for her car keys on the way. She unlocked the door, scrambled inside, and quickly locked the door behind her. Then she rocked back and forth until she was finally calm again. It was the last time she went to one of her daughter's soccer games.

People who have panic attacks are afraid of having further attacks. The sensation of being out of control—pounding heart, hyperventilating, sweating, and going numb—is so overwhelming that they do almost anything to avoid feeling that way again. For some, it means avoiding places that bring on attacks. For others, it means avoiding anyplace where escape is difficult. Eventually, people with agoraphobia can't leave the house unless they are with a "safe" person—someone on whom they rely to keep them calm.

Someone who can't leave the safety of his or her home is said to be suffering from panic attacks with agoraphobia. The person who is still willing to go out is said to suffer from panic attacks without agoraphobia.

It is important that you not confuse agoraphobia with

an actual phobia. Agoraphobia describes a person's inability to leave his or her home. In contrast, as we will see in the next chapter, a phobia is an exaggerated fear of a specific event or situation.

Nocturnal Panic Attacks

It is also possible to experience panic attacks when you sleep. My father suffered from nocturnal panic attacks. Every so often, he'd wake up in the middle of the night feeling as if he were suffocating. His heart would be pounding, his pulse racing, and his fingers and toes would feel tingly and numb. Thinking he was having a heart attack, he'd jump out of bed. But after making it to the bathroom without incident, he'd realize it was one of his "spells." He'd return to bed without further trouble once the adrenaline dissipated through his body.

Nocturnal panic attacks are not uncommon. In these cases, the body's alarm is inexplicably triggered and the SNS is activated. People seem to stop having these attacks by the time they reach their sixties.

A panic attack, whether nocturnal or not, lasts only ten to twenty minutes. The symptoms gradually diminish when the PNS kicks in.

Panic and Post-Traumatic Stress Disorder

Jonathan saw both his brothers gunned down in a drive-by shooting in front of his house. Now, whenever he sees slow-moving cars driving through his neighborhood, he has a panic attack.

Rachel Green was sexually abused by her stepfather from the age of six until the time she left home, at age sixteen. Every night she lay in bed, dreading the sound of her father's footsteps coming down the hall. Now in her late teens, she can't sleep unless all the lights are on in the apartment.

Tracy witnessed a horrible car accident while she was waiting to cross the street. A truck crashed into a car waiting to make a left turn, and the car's occupant was thrown through the windshield. Now Tracy suffers from nightmares and panic attacks. She sees the body fly through the windshield over and over.

When he was only seven years old, Marcus escaped a fire that burned his house to the ground; his younger brother died in his crib because no one could get back into the burning building to save him. Sometimes in the middle of the night, Marcus can still hear his brother's cries. To this day, Marcus can't stand the smell of fire and refuses to live in a house that has a fireplace.

What do these four people have in common? They all suffer from post-traumatic stress disorder (PTSD). A trauma is any event outside the normal range of human experience. People who have been sexually abused, or who have witnessed natural disasters (such as tornadoes, fires, and floods) or man-made disasters (such as shootings, car accidents, and kidnappings), have all been through traumas.

People who suffer from PTSD show three major symptoms: hypervigilance (being on guard at all times), intrusion (thinking about the trauma, having nightmares), and constriction (limiting their lifestyle to avoid thinking about the trauma). The hypervigilance and intrusion lead to panic attacks, and the constriction may lead to agoraphobia as the person tries to avoid situations reminiscent of the trauma.

When people start to avoid certain situations, they're often on their way to developing phobias, which are the focus of the next chapter.

Phobias, Social Phobia, and Obsessive-Compulsive Disorder

Tonya

Tonya was relaxing in a bubble bath. She put the book she was reading on the floormat and slid down into the warm, sudsy water. Suddenly out of the corner of her eye she saw something move.

A spider. Tonya bolted upright and screamed. "Kill it; kill it!" But no one was home.

She froze. Maybe she should leave it alone, she thought. But then it would be there whenever she used the bathroom. Or it might crawl into her room at night.

She looked around for a weapon. Spying her shoe within arm's reach, she made a tentative move. She edged her hand toward the shoe, keeping an eye on the spider. Her heart was pounding, and even in the warm water she felt an icy coldness sweeping through her body.

Her fingers touched the shoe and pulled it toward her. Slowly, she eased herself out of the tub. Trying to decide how to approach it, she stared at the spider. Finally, she threw the shoe; the spider sped across the cabinet door and scooted inside.

Tonya screamed again. She grabbed her towel and raced out of the room. Her heart was still pounding and she was having trouble breathing. She couldn't help but think the spider was plotting the quickest route to her bedroom.

The rest of the afternoon, Tonya stayed away from the bathroom. The water in the tub had grown cold. Tonya felt silly for letting a stupid little spider scare her away, but she just couldn't bring herself to go back in there. When her brother came home, she sent him in to find it and kill it.

A phobia is an excessive, long-lasting fear of something specific. Tonya clearly was phobic about spiders. Phobias are often related to panic attacks because a person experiences the same set of symptoms when exposed to the thing he or she dreads as he or she does in a panic attack.

Simple Phobias

When people are afraid of specific things, and the fear is actually disproportionate to the situation, they are said to be suffering from simple phobias. They aren't truly phobic, however, until they start avoiding, or wanting to avoid, the thing that frightens them.

A fear is not a phobia unless you have to alter your whole life to avoid coming into contact with that which you fear. Your excessive attempts to avoid something make living a normal life increasingly difficult.

People are phobic about various things. Common phobias include a fear of heights, snakes, spiders, dogs, strangers, dentists and doctors, or water. Often, simple phobias result from traumatic experiences. Kids who

13

were bitten by dogs often grow up to be phobic about dogs. People injured in car accidents are sometimes phobic about driving again. A client of mine is phobic about water. She never swims, and she'll go for days without taking a bath or shower. One day she told me why: Her mother had tried to drown her in the bathtub when she was a little girl.

Many people are uncomfortable around certain things. This does not necessarily mean they have a phobia. I may not like the dentist, but I still go regularly. A fear is not a phobia unless you have to alter your life in order to manage the fear.

Social Phobias

When I was in high school, I developed difficulty swallowing. Every time I tried to eat I felt as if I'd lost the ability to swallow. Instead of swallowing, I would gag. It was particularly bad in public, so I avoided any occasions where I would have to eat in company.

On one occasion, I was asked to attend a Father/Daughter banquet with an old family friend. I thought I'd be okay because I knew this man well; besides, the dinner was just a small part of the evening.

I was having a great time until the food was served. With the very first mouthful, I couldn't swallow. My face flushed; the room was suddenly too hot, but my hands felt cold and clammy. I thought I was choking, and I gagged as I tried to force down the food.

Was everyone looking at me? I couldn't spit the food out; I was mortified. What if I got sick? I was breathing faster now and feeling a little dizzy. What if I passed out right here? How far away was the hospital?

Miraculously, I finally swallowed the food. Relief swept over me and I felt my face cool down—until I scooped up the next forkful. Panic set in again. I repeated the whole procedure: try to swallow, gag, try again to swallow, gag some more, finally swallow and breathe.

The only thing I can say for the dinner is that I survived it, and eventually they came and took away my plate. I was quite relaxed and happy after that.

I had a social phobia—a fear of embarrassing myself in public. I didn't learn until many years later that this condition has a name, and that social phobias are very common among teenagers. Fear of choking is the second most common form of social phobia. The first is fear of speaking in public.

Although social phobias frequently begin in late childhood and extend into a person's early twenties, most people seem to outgrow them. Social phobias differ from simple phobias in that the real fear is of embarrassing yourself. People may be afraid of using the bathroom, eating, using the telephone, or even signing their name in public. People who suffer from social phobias typically fear being observed, thinking that others are laughing at them or finding fault with them. As a result, they start avoiding places where they may feel these things are happening.

How can you tell if a person has agoraphobia or a social phobia? If the person avoids going to the mall or the grocery store out of fear of doing something embarrassing, the person has a social phobia. If the person avoids going to those same places because he or she is afraid of having a panic attack, he or she suffers from agoraphobia.

Some people who have panic attacks develop phobias. They experience a panic attack and then try to find a logical explanation for it. If they panicked while driving down the highway, they associate the panic attack with the highway. Then they avoid driving on the highway. The avoidance reinforces the fear and contributes to the development of a phobia. Since avoidance brings relief, you are encouraged to run away from your fear. By running away, you are telling yourself that the fearful situation is too overwhelming for you to handle. As a result, the phobia grows.

Obsessive-Compulsive Disorder

Obsessive-compulsive disorder means having persistent, distressing thoughts and repeating either certain behaviors (like handwashing or checking) or mental acts (like praying or counting) to cancel out these thoughts.

Mike

Mike had just obtained his driver's license and was driving home from work one night. On a desolate stretch of road, he thought to himself that it was a place he'd sure hate to have a flat tire. Within minutes, he began to worry that something was wrong with his back tire. He finally pulled over and got out to check. Both back tires looked fine. As he put the

16

car in gear again, he had the nagging suspicion that something was really wrong with the tire. He grabbed the flashlight again and took one more look at the tire.

Angry with himself, he got back into the car. "I really hate being out here like this," he muttered.

He hadn't driven more than a quarter of a mile when he felt an overwhelming need to check the tire again. But this time, he wondered if the problem was really with the tire. Maybe he had run over something—or maybe someone. He got out and examined the tires carefully, but there was no sign of blood or punctures.

Still, maybe he should go back and look along the side of the road. Maybe someone was lying there right now, bleeding to death.

He turned the car around and checked along the side of the road. Nothing. Once again, he started back home. A mile down the road, he again had to turn around and check "just one more time." In the end, it took him an additional hour and a half to make it home from work. Each night he worked, Mike had trouble driving home without stopping about twenty times to check whether he had driven over someone. He didn't dare tell anyone what was going on, for fear they'd think he was crazy. Then he began to wonder if indeed he was crazy.

Mike wasn't crazy, although he felt as if he were at the mercy of his strange compulsion to check. He suffered from obsessive-compulsive disorder. This often starts in adolescence, particularly in boys.

17

Donna

Donna had a strong fear of saying something horrible and inappropriate in math class. Whenever the teacher called on students for answers, Donna sank down into her seat. She was terrified that the teacher would call on her and that instead of stating the answer, she would blurt out, "You look fat in that dress" or "I can't stop staring at your huge nose." Donna worried so much about saying something awful to her teacher that she could barely concentrate on the lessons.

At lunch, Donna sat alone because she feared that she would say something horrible to someone. Maybe she'd tell the head cheerleader that her recent dye job had frizzed her hair; maybe she'd tell the captain of the football team that he had flabby arms. Lately, being around people made Donna nervous because she never knew what would spill out of her mouth. Her solution was to begin skipping class and avoiding people. The obsessive thoughts only went away when people weren't around or she was alone with her family at home.

As you can tell from the name, obsessive-compulsive disorder has two distinct parts: obsessions and compulsions. Obsessions are thoughts that won't go away. They are unwanted, uncontrollable, and often inappropriate thoughts, such as thinking you might stab someone with a knife that's lying on the kitchen counter. Compulsions then develop in response to obsessions. Repeating certain physical or mental tasks over and over helps to buy some relief from the anxiety of the obsession.

Everyone has inappropriate thoughts from time to time, and everyone has routines, but someone is said to have obsessive-compulsive disorder when a routine interferes with the rest of his or her life.

The most common compulsion is checking. Some people check to see if they have turned off the stove, turned out the lights, or locked the front door. They don't just check once or twice; they may check twenty or thirty times. Other people have compulsions to touch things, certain rituals for walking through doorways, or certain ways of getting dressed for school or work each day. Failing to perform their rituals brings them excruciating discomfort.

Their reasoning, which is sometimes called "magical thinking," goes like this: "If I perform this ritual right or say something five times in a row, nothing bad will happen to me (or to a loved one)." The fear that something bad will happen drives the person with OCD to perform rituals over and over until he or she "feels" that they have been done correctly.

The rituals or litanies (spoken phrases) are usually connected to the obsessive worries in some way. Someone who constantly fears doing something blasphemous (anti-religious) may pray compulsively; someone who is obsessed with contamination may compulsively wash his or her hands. In some cases, the connection between the obsessions and the compulsions may not be obvious or logical to anyone other than the person with OCD.

Ordinary Anxiety

All people feel anxiety at some time. That's normal. A shy teenager who doesn't want to give a speech in class doesn't necessarily have a social phobia. The little boy who worries endlessly that his father is going to die during open-heart surgery doesn't necessarily have obsessive-compulsive disorder.

In the face of danger, the panic response is normal. Anxiety is also normal, signaling us to take a look at the stress in our lives. Only when these symptoms—panic and anxiety—become so crippling that we can't continue our daily patterns do we have a disorder that needs to be treated.

Part II:
What Causes These Disorders?

It's a Chemical Thing ...

Panic Attacks

Panic attacks happen for a variety of reasons. Often they result from a combination of emotional and physical factors, with one setting off the other. Humans were designed so that danger activates the fight or flight response, which originates in the brain. Things can go awry, however. Any malfunction in the brain, especially in the region of the lower brain called the locus ceruleus (which controls our emotional responses), can cause panic symptoms. Scientists have discovered that they can induce panic symptoms by stimulating this region electrically; they can also disrupt a panic attack by administering drugs or damaging the locus ceruleus.

Several different situations can set off panic symptoms in the locus ceruleus. If you are extremely sensitive to carbon dioxide, you may react with panic symptoms when too much carbon dioxide is in your body. This may happen because of hyperventilation—breathing too fast and too shallowly. People who are anxious tend to hyperventilate, and hyperventilating leads to a buildup of carbon dioxide circulating in the system. Carbon dioxide buildup also may happen after vigorous exercise.

There is a connection between the locus ceruleus and

the quantity of neurotransmitters in that region, as well. Neurotransmitters are chemicals secreted by the neurons, or brain cells, which enable other neurons to work together. Sometimes insufficient or excessive neurotransmitters (in this case, norepinephrine and serotonin) cause the locus ceruleus to go haywire. This sets off an unnecessary panic attack. That is why certain antidepressant medications that directly affect the quantity of norepinephrine and serotonin help to prevent panic attacks.

Anxiety States

There are several generally accepted biological causes of anxiety. The first is that people feel anxious because they have an insufficient amount of the neurotransmitter gamma aminobutyric acid, or GABA. GABA is associated with calming the brain. It actually works by inhibiting neurons that would ordinarily set off the alarm, so that high levels (or at least sufficient levels) of GABA help keep a person calm.

Anxiety can also result from artificially stimulating the body. Drugs such as caffeine, nicotine, amphetamines, and cocaine all provoke an anxiety reaction.

One of my clients came in complaining of severe anxiety and frequent panic attacks. Dorothy worked as a data entry operator. As I probed into what kinds of stress she might be encountering at work, I learned that she was actually bored with her job. In fact, she was so bored that she had to drink ten cups of coffee a day just to keep awake.

Ten cups of coffee!? The woman was consuming enormous amounts of caffeine! Once she decreased her

23

coffee consumption to one cup a day, she no longer experienced anxiety.

Certain medical conditions can cause symptoms of anxiety and panic as well. In fact, more than fifty physical conditions cause anxiety. If a doctor is not careful to treat the primary medical condition, he or she may not be able to cure the anxiety. Endocrine disorders, such as diabetes and hypoglycemia, cause many of the same symptoms as those of panic attacks. Hyperthyroidism or inner ear disturbances may cause anxiety symptoms to develop as well.

A relatively harmless heart condition called mitral valve prolapse can be another trigger. In some people's hearts, the mitral valve does not fully close after blood has passed from one chamber into another. This leads to a small backflow of blood, which is essentially harmless but can cause some uncomfortable sensations. A person with mitral valve prolapse may feel his or her heart beat an extra beat or pound a little harder than usual. This usually goes away with no harm done. However, people may interpret these erratic heartbeats as the beginning of a panic attack or heart attack. If they react with alarm, their anxiety level increases and they may indeed suffer a panic attack (although they will not suffer a heart attack).

People often suffer from panic attacks after major heart surgery. They confuse the pounding heart or occasional irregular beat with a pending heart attack. Fearful of dying, they react with anxiety and set a panic attack in motion.

Other medical conditions are not causes of anxiety but become larger problems because of anxiety. People sometimes say that asthma attacks can be brought on by anxiety.

Actually, that's only partially correct—someone can't bring on an asthma attack if he or she doesn't have the condition in the first place. But anxiety can aggravate symptoms in someone who is already asthmatic.

Tourette's syndrome is another condition worsened by anxiety. Tourette's is a neurological condition that resembles obsessive-compulsive disorder in that its sufferers feel compelled to do certain things to relieve their anxiety. Unfortunately, what they often feel compelled to do is curse and yell inappropriate words in public. People afflicted with Tourette's feel immeasurable pressure to do these unpleasant things. If they refrain, they only feel more anxious. The anxiety, then, is both a by-product of the condition and a contributor to it.

Sleep disorders are made worse by anxiety. People who are feeling anxious often don't sleep well. Some people sleepwalk; others suffer from insomnia.

Finally, certain medications can provoke anxiety as a side effect. Sometimes even the medications that are designed to treat anxiety cause anxiety. People who have become addicted to a class of tranquilizers called benzodiazepines experience symptoms of anxiety when they stop taking the medication. In fact, as people stop using most drugs, including alcohol, they experience many symptoms of anxiety.

Obsessive-Compulsive Disorder

Doctors have recognized that people with obsessive-compulsive disorder may have a chemical imbalance. They may suffer from unusually low levels of the neurotransmitter serotonin. Serotonin affects memory, sleep, appetite, mood, and the ability to refrain from repetitive actions. Medications known to increase levels of serotonin allow the person suffering from obsessive-compulsive disorder to behave normally again.

Environmental Toxins

Finally, certain environmental toxins, such as insecticides, mercury, and lead, can cause panic attacks. These toxins affect the brain, thus activating the alarm system.

Although there is a physiological basis for many panic attacks, as well as a possible genetic component (because anxiety disorders tend to run in families), other factors, such as stress and how a person reacts to stress, play a role. We'll explore these factors in the next chapter.

It's Too Much Stress ...

Sometimes the way we react to stressful situations causes us to develop symptoms of anxiety.

Francine

At sixteen, Francine had her share of situational stress. Her parents were divorced and her mother worked two jobs to keep the bills paid. As the eldest of six children, it was up to Francine to see that her brothers and sisters got to school on time, ate decent meals, and stayed out of trouble.

Francine took her role seriously. She planned meals, cooked and cleaned, and helped her siblings with their homework as much as she could. When any of the kids had trouble at school, Francine handled it; she thought her mother was too tired to take care of such things.

Francine thought she was handling everything well, but managing a household of seven when you're only sixteen and a kid yourself is a pretty big burden. She started getting stomachaches and headaches. She used over-the-counter medicines to treat her physical problems, but as her brothers and sisters got older, the situational stress got worse. Some of them didn't do their homework, and they didn't like Francine forcing them to do it—she was only their sister, after all. And once they found boyfriends and girlfriends, they resented Francine sticking her nose in their business.

Francine suffered her first panic attack when she was seventeen. She was sitting in sixth period, trying to concentrate on the subject at hand, when she suddenly felt faint. She put her head down for a moment, thinking the feeling would go away, but it got worse instead. Her face flushed and she could hear her heart pounding away. It felt like it was going to break right through her chest. "Oh my God!" she thought. "I'm going to die!" Francine jumped up and bolted for the door. No time to explain. She had to get some air.

Once in the hall, she leaned against a locker, trying to catch her breath. She still felt too hot, so she opened a side door and ran out. She walked around the grounds for a few moments, calming herself. "What's wrong with me?" she wondered. "Am I having a heart attack?"

Francine was experiencing the classic signs of a panic attack. In this case, her inability to deal with all of her situational stress—her family responsibilities—had contributed to the formation of an anxiety disorder. Too much emotional stress and too few resources to manage it left Francine vulnerable to anxiety.

A former client of mine had chronic anxiety because she worked for a boss who expected her to do the work of three people. Michelle didn't complain because she needed the job, and she was afraid that he would replace her. However, it was impossible for her to accomplish all that her boss expected. So she kept going to work, although she dreaded it, and every time she was late for a deadline, she popped a tranquilizer to calm her nerves.

She didn't recognize that her symptoms of anxiety stemmed from her inability to stand up for herself or set appropriate boundaries. As long as she neglected her feelings, she felt stressed and anxious.

Stressful situations contribute to anxiety, but if people learn to deal effectively with them (as discussed in chapter 6), they don't have to let their symptoms of anxiety turn into full-fledged anxiety disorders.

Traumatic Events

Some people believe that trauma causes biological changes within the brain. Although that is certainly possible, it has not been proven conclusively. More people believe that trauma works on an emotional level to cause anxiety and panic.

Consider Shawn, whose home was wiped out by a tornado. Now every time there's a thunderstorm, Shawn has a panic attack. The darkening sky, the roaring winds, and even the bulletins on television remind him of the time he hid in his closet while a tornado ravaged his neighborhood.

Shawn had been terrified that night. But because the threat was real—his life was in danger—the panic made sense. Now, although the panic persists, the danger is not real anymore. Yes, thunderstorms can cause a lot of damage, but most don't involve tornadoes. And Shawn, who has convinced himself that he's always in danger, suffers unnecessarily. His reaction to the traumatic event has created the anxiety and panic.

A friend of mine was bitten by a dog when she was a child. Now Cynthia is afraid of all dogs, even the slow, sweet basset hound that lives next door. Being around any dog causes her to start shaking, her heart to start pounding, and her stomach to turn over. Most of the dogs she comes in contact with are friendly and obedient. However, the memory of that early attack so traumatized her that she reacts with undue anxiety every time.

Tornado Trauma

On May 3, 1999, Oklahoma City was ravaged by an F5 tornado (the most dangerous type of tornado known today). Dean Hoppe and his wife Laura huddled in a closet on the first floor of their home, which stood directly in the tornado's path. They had sought cover when they realized that the tornado was not going to change direction.

As they huddled in the closet, they could smell the dirt in the air even though they'd closed and secured all their windows. Suddenly the power went out. Then they heard the deafening roar of the tornado, like a freight train bearing down on their house. The windows blew out; dirt and rain swirled around and the contents of their house were sucked into the air. A few moments later, Dean realized that the house was rising up off of its foundation.

Although the storm seemed to last an eternity, it was over in minutes. Miraculously, the closet had been left intact. When Dean and Laura opened the door, they could see the sky overhead—the whole second floor of their home had been swept away by the storm.

Dean and Laura survived, unhurt, though their home was considered a total loss. But for nights after the tornado, Dean re-lived the terror over and over again in his dreams, hearing the approaching high winds, smelling the dirt in the air, feeling the lifting of the house around him.

Phobias and Primitive Fears

Some researchers theorize that there's a reason why many people have phobic reactions to snakes and spiders. Since some snakes and spiders are poisonous, they believe that we are programmed to fear them. In primitive times, panicking and running away from snakes probably saved many lives.

Unfortunately, nowadays some of us sense that same urgency when faced with a harmless garter snake or spider. We react with panic without first assessing the danger. It's not that we've even been bitten before; we simply feel uneasy, and consequently we panic. Trauma hasn't programmed us to run from these creatures; our uneasiness, which might be a holdover response from earlier times, has programmed us.

Perfectionist Parents

Some people are more anxious than others because they've been raised by perfectionist parents. Parents who have extremely high standards of achievement may have children who drive themselves excessively to try to meet these impossible expectations.

One person I know had to clean her room every night before she could go to bed. Dirty clothes had to be stashed in the hamper, and nothing could be hidden under the bed. Everything was supposed to be hung in her closet facing a certain direction. If anything was askew, her father would get her out of bed (no matter what time of night) and make her rehang the offending article of clothing. Not surprisingly, this anxious young woman went on to develop obsessive-compulsive disorder.

Another young woman developed a social phobia. Her mother was extremely critical of her, finding fault with the way she looked, her grades, and her ability to make friends. Sharon's father had left the family when Sharon was very young. By the time she was a teenager, Sharon had concluded that he had left because he couldn't stand her mother's tirades.

But Sharon couldn't leave; she had no place to go. Not only that, she was attached to her mother. Her self-esteem plummeted. As an awkward teenager, Sharon started feeling more and more nervous whenever she was the center of any attention. She almost fainted the day she had to give a speech in class and she talked herself out of trying out for a softball team because too many people would be watching her.

Social phobias often develop in children raised in rigid households or by parents who are social phobics themselves. If some children develop phobias like those of their parents, it may be because they have copied the behavior they saw at home. Perhaps it has more to do with observation and imitation than with genetics. Not surprisingly, anxious parents have anxious kids.

Anticipatory Anxiety

The true panic attack comes from out of the blue. More than likely, there is a biological reason for it. But because the symptoms are so frightening, and the event is so unpredictable, the panic victim begins to fear having another one. The way she feels—nervous, sweaty palms, stomach tied in knots—is called anticipatory anxiety. In other words, she is anticipating having another panic attack at any moment, and is constantly on guard. Medication may exist to stop a panic attack from occurring, but the same medication does little to stop the buildup of anxiety.

Anticipatory anxiety comes from not knowing how to deal with the panic situation. You may talk yourself into a worse reaction, or you rely on people or substances to make you feel safe. Let's look at some of the ways we make small problems bigger.

Avoidance

Avoidance is the quickest way to convert a fear into a phobia. Whether you have been traumatized or have associated your first panic attack with a specific situation, once you start avoiding those situations, you make the fear worse because you have not faced it. When you change your lifestyle to accommodate the fear, you have created a phobia. So, whether or not a phobia has a biological basis, emotional factors (the way we think about the event and the subsequent way we behave) maintain the phobia.

For example, I happen to dislike scorpions. I've only seen a few in my life, and fortunately most of them were in the zoo. Because I live in Oklahoma, however, I have to consider that I'll probably run into one at some point.

I don't know why I'm so frantic around scorpions. Their sting is rarely fatal, although it can make you very sick. I never considered my feelings about scorpions to be phobic. I thought they made perfect sense.

That was the case until a dear friend bought a house in the country. It's a beautiful house with enormous, sunny rooms and many windows. It's cozy, with plants in every room and, unfortunately, a few scorpions here and there.

"Don't worry," my friend said. "If you see one, just step on it."

Just step on a scorpion? I'd sooner run in front of a speeding car.

I have visited my friend twice at her new house. The first time I was very uncomfortable because I kept expecting an army of scorpions to march in from the porch. I hung out in the kitchen because the stools were high, and if I climbed up on them, my feet didn't touch the floor. I felt safer there.

When she asked me to come sit with other guests in

the living room, I froze. What if a scorpion was out there, hiding under a plant? Can scorpions smell fear?

I cut that first visit short. The second visit was even worse. Several guests wanted to walk around the yard and down to the creek. I was paralyzed. There was no way that I was going to walk outside when scorpions were around. So they went without me, leaving me alone in the house. I stood there feeling queasy. Then I made a run for the kitchen and climbed up on a stool. By the time they returned, I was ready to go home.

That was the last time I visited my friend. I never did encounter a scorpion, but the mere possibility haunted me. I've made myself more afraid by avoiding the place and not confronting my fear. That's what I mean when I say phobias become worse depending on what message we give ourselves. Avoidance is a strong message that some situations are too dangerous to face.

Reliance on Medication

Some people have another method of handling stressful situations. When they start feeling anxious, they pop a pill or smoke a marijuana joint. Many alcoholics start drinking because they are afraid of social encounters. Fearing a situation in which they might have a panic attack, they rely on a substance—such as alcohol, tranquilizers, or illegal drugs—or another person to get them through the situation. If they do this often enough, they associate relief from anxiety with taking the drug or having that particular person with them. Soon enough, they become unable to face the situation without the drug or the person to serve as a safety net.

Reliance on safety nets works the same way as avoidance. Avoiding the source of your fears brings relief, so avoidance becomes a way of life. Likewise, turning to drugs can become a way of life because initially it brings relief from the fear. In addition, having a safety net becomes problematic because you learn you can't handle the situation alone.

A client of mine named Lawrence had been taking three times the amount of tranquilizer prescribed by his primary care doctor. Apparently he had been going to several doctors and getting prescriptions from all of them. Even worse, some of the doctors did not keep track of how many pills they ordered.

By the time I inherited the case, Lawrence had relied so much on his tranquilizers that he had grown addicted to them and had lost faith that he could play any role in defeating anxiety himself.

Self-Talk

It isn't always an event that causes the panic. More often than not, it's our self-talk—what we tell ourselves about a situation—that makes the situation worse.

One day one of my clients called me, sounding out of breath.

"I need to go to the hospital," she said, gasping for air. "And I want them to know you're my therapist so that you can tell them what kind of medicine would be best for me to take."

"Sara, is that you?" I asked. I had never heard her so upset.

"I think something's really wrong," she continued. "I

think I need to be hospitalized. I might even be having a heart attack."

"Slow down, Sara " I said. "Tell me what's going on."

"Well, I was at work, and all of a sudden I started to feel really hot. That didn't make sense because the air conditioner was going full blast. Anyway," she said, pausing for more air, "I fanned myself a little and then started feeling dizzy. I sat down and realized that my heart was pounding. It felt as if it was about to explode right there in my chest. I told my boss I was having a heart attack and that I was going to the emergency room. Then I called you."

"It sounds as if you're having a panic attack," I said.

"But my hands feel all tingly, and I think I'm going to faint," she cried, still breathing hard.

"That's because you're hyperventilating," I said. "Do you have a paper bag handy?"

"I have one right here," she replied.

"Okay, then start breathing into the bag right now."

I heard her put the bag to her face and start breathing into it. After a minute or so, her breathing became slower. She got back on the phone. "I'm breathing better," she said.

"Good," I said. "You're having a panic attack. A panic attack lasts anywhere from ten to twenty minutes; you can ride it out. If you know what's happening, you won't over-react. When you're a little calmer, come out here. We'll talk about panic attacks."

Sara agreed, and indeed she was feeling calmer by the time I saw her.

Had I not known that she had a history of panic attacks,

I might have wondered about a heart attack, too. Fortunately, Sara simply needed to learn how to talk herself through one of these panics. Her method had been to talk herself into a bigger panic. If a biological reason prompted the first attack, her negative self-talk kept the panic growing.

What do I mean by "self-talk"? Sara would start to feel a panic attack coming on, but instead of telling herself that she could ride out the symptoms, she would think things like: "Oh, this is awful. I don't think I can handle this. What if I'm really having a heart attack this time? Can I make it to the hospital in time? Maybe I'll die this time. Maybe I won't, but I'll probably never get better. I can't live like this for another twenty years."

By the time the person finishes scaring herself, her anxiety has caused the panic attack to last longer than it would have without the negative commentary. Clearly, negative self-talk feeds anxiety and makes the symptoms worse. A better alternative is positive self-talk, which I'll talk about later in this book.

Conflict over Aggressive Impulses

Anxiety may also arise from the battle between our impulses—the things that we want to do—and our social conscience—the things that we know society will permit us to do. This theory originated with Sigmund Freud, a renowned Viennese psychologist who thought that people grew anxious because they were afraid that they might do something that was considered inappropriate by society.

For example, Lamont lived with a stepfather. Sometimes

his stepfather treated him well, but more often than not, he was abusive. Lamont hated his stepfather, but he also tried very hard to win his stepfather's respect.

When Lamont was fifteen, he started dreaming about killing his stepfather. He would wake up in a cold sweat, incredulous that he could have dreamed up such violence. He also started worrying about sharp instruments being left around the house. He hid all the knives in the linen closet and buried the scissors in the bottom of a kitchen drawer. He hated falling asleep for fear he would dream again.

After a few months, Lamont started worrying that someone would break into his parents' house. He kept getting out of bed to check that all the doors were locked. Eventually, his checking took over more and more of his time.

Lamont continually struggled with his own feelings and urges. He developed an anxiety about knives and scissors because he feared that he might use one of these objects to harm his stepfather. He also feared that someone would break into the house and kill his stepfather—which could be seen as a fulfillment of Lamont's wish.

Is Anxiety Biological or Emotional?

Anxiety can stem from either physical or emotional causes, or a combination of both. Even when we don't know the cause, it is wise to consider a physical cause first, since physical causes are usually easier to treat. However, it's just as likely that emotional factors are contributing to a person's anxiety, and those often take longer to treat. Changing one's reaction to stressful situations and learning to tolerate uncomfortable symptoms and to talk more positively takes a great deal of effort. That is what we'll look at later in this book. Anxiety and its disorders are treatable no matter what the cause.

The Consequences
of Anxiety

Terri

Terri had been listening to her parents fight for the past several days. She tried not to listen, but it was hard to ignore two people shouting at each other and slamming things around. There had been days of fighting before, but this seemed more serious and Terri wished it would stop.

She turned off the television and went into her bedroom, closing the door behind her. Her stomach was on fire, even though she had only eaten soup for supper. She lay down on the bed and tried to relax. Her stomach began to churn, and Terri knew she was going to be sick. She hoped her parents wouldn't hear her.

After vomiting, she wiped her face and saw droplets of blood around her mouth. Startled, she looked into the toilet and saw more blood. Should she tell her parents? Should she see a doctor?

Terri sat back on her heels on the cold bathroom floor. Something was really wrong this time. She had always had a nervous stomach, but throwing up blood was new. She clutched her stomach. It really hurt. Maybe she had cancer. Terri crawled back to her room, grabbed the heating pad, and tried to relax, but she still felt sick to her stomach.

The truth is, Terri didn't have cancer. She had the beginnings of an ulcer, a very painful condition in which the acidic juices of the stomach start eating a hole in the stomach wall. Clearly, it's a condition that requires medical treatment. And it is often a result of constant feelings of anxiety.

Physical Consequences

When you are anxious, your body and mind are primed for danger. When the danger is over, your body returns to normal. However, if you are chronically anxious, you feel that the danger is never over. You remain on guard. Your sympathetic nervous system is activated most of the time, and that takes a toll on your body.

In general, anxious people have a lot of physical complaints. There are two main reasons for this. First, anxious people are tense, and muscle tension can lead to injury and chronic pain. Second, anxious people have weakened immune systems because of the ongoing physical stress of heightened alertness. Weakened immune systems make people more likely to get sick. They catch colds more easily because their bodies are less able to fight off infections.

Muscle tension leads to chronic pain. Tense people, especially those who hold in their anger, often complain that their shoulders ache. Many complain of lower-back problems that ultimately make back injuries more likely.

Anxious people feel aches and pains all over their bodies because it hurts to be so rigid all the time. In addition, most are not even aware that they are rigid, which makes it hard to correct the problem.

Ulcers are often a result of chronic anxiety. When you're anxious, your stomach secretes more acid, and the acid can eat a hole in your stomach wall.

Irritable bowel syndrome is another anxiety-worsened disorder. Instead of the stomach, the colon is affected. People with irritable bowel syndrome suffer from alternating bouts of diarrhea and constipation. The syndrome can progress to ulcerative colitis if an ulcerated area starts to grow in the colon wall.

Bruxism develops when people grind or clench their teeth. This may happen when people are angry or afraid, especially if they are holding in these feelings. Grinding puts pounds of pressure on the teeth enamel and on the bone surrounding the teeth. It doesn't take long for the constant wear and tear to crack a tooth, chip off enamel, or cause the bone to break down.

Anxious people see doctors frequently. They catch more viruses, are injury-prone, and have frequent headaches and stomach trouble. Anxious people are not all hypochondriacs—people who make up their illnesses. Most of the time, these people really are sick, and usually their anxiety has contributed to their illnesses.

Sleep Disorders

Anxiety can also contribute to sleep disorders. People who have suffered traumatic events often experience recurrent nightmares and night terrors. Nightmares and night terrors are both linked to anxiety, but they occur during different levels of sleep. When you fall asleep, your body goes through four levels of sleep. Stage I is the lightest level of sleep; stage IV is the deepest and most restorative to the body. After you have been in stage IV sleep for about thirty minutes, you start to rouse from this deep state and slip back into a lighter sleep. You go up through stage III to stage II sleep.

This cycle happens throughout the night. These four stages of sleep comprise NREM (non-rapid eye movement) sleep, during which the brain does not typically engage in dreaming. You pass through each night drifting in and out of stages II and III, spending less and less time in stage IV.

Between the stages is another kind of sleep: REM (rapid eye movement) sleep. This is when you dream. REM sleep is believed to be mentally restorative; without it, you would be edgy and irritable all the time. The REM periods get longer throughout the night. By morning, you're spending much more time in REM.

Nightmares occur during REM sleep, so they frequently occur later in the sleep cycle. Nightmares are bad dreams. You wake up and usually remember the dream all too well. You're afraid and may call out to someone for comfort. You know where you are and what's going on. Nightmares happen more often to those people who are under a lot of stress, or have suffered trauma, because they are using all their energy during the day to keep thoughts of the trauma at bay. When they fall asleep, their guard is down. Memories come back in the form of bad dreams.

Night terrors happen during NREM sleep. They are not

dreams, or at least not the type of dream with a story-line. When you are in stage IV sleep, you are very relaxed. If someone tried to wake you, it would be difficult. As you return to the lighter stage III sleep, you sometimes have difficulty making the transition. If you are overtired or are under a lot of stress, your body resists coming out of stage IV, and you wake up—but you don't really wake up, you just appear to be awake. You remember any scary image or thought that preceded this waking up, and you scream in terror. You may thrash around or fall off the bed.

If you try to calm a person who has had a night terror, you only succeed in scaring him more because he doesn't know where he is or who you are. In the morning, he won't remember the event at all. In fact, when left alone, the person with a night terror returns to sleep.

Sleepwalking is similar to night terrors. Anxious people are more likely to sleepwalk, especially when they're older.

Finally, anxious people tend to have trouble getting to sleep. They suffer from insomnia—an inability either to fall asleep or stay asleep. For example, people with symptoms of obsessive-compulsive compulsive disorder worry a lot, and nighttime is when many do the most worrying. Obviously, dwelling on the same thought hour after hour will keep you from falling asleep and having a restful night. People who have nocturnal panic attacks or nightmares may fear falling asleep.

Unfortunately, people who don't get adequate sleep become anxious and irritable. The anxiety that may have contributed to the sleeping problem in the first place now becomes worse—a by-product of the sleeping problem.

Panic and Your Long-Term Health

Panic attacks may wear you down, but they won't kill you. Panic attacks do not inevitably become heart attacks. You won't go crazy from having panic symptoms, and you won't have a stroke. In fact, you can adjust to panic symptoms, even though they can be extremely uncomfortable.

The problem isn't really the panic attacks. The anticipatory anxiety that accompanies panic attacks is much harder on your health. Panic attacks are time-limited; your body has a built-in mechanism to calm you after ten to twenty minutes. However, anticipatory anxiety lasts longer, and that can be damaging to your health. As anxiety weakens your body, it can create the climate for the onset of other diseases, like heart disease or cancer, that you may be genetically prone to. That's why treatment of anxiety is so important—and this is the subject of the next section of this book.

Part III:
Managing Everyday Anxiety

Self-Help
Techniques

Our society is a stressful one. Although many of you will not go on to develop full-fledged anxiety disorders, you will undoubtedly be subjected to many stressful situations. The good news is that you can learn ways to handle these situations. If you understand how stress creates anxiety, and you can effectively manage your reaction to that stress, you are less likely to develop an anxiety disorder. If you already have an anxiety disorder, you can learn more effective ways to manage the stress around you.

Ten Ways to Manage Stress

1. Learn to recognize the signs of internal stress: the butterflies in your stomach, the pounding heart, the muscle tension. Practice relaxation techniques to calm yourself, and learn how to problem-solve so that small problems don't grow into big ones.

Relaxation techniques: Practice progressively tensing and relaxing all the muscles of your body. Start with your hand. Make a fist and clench as hard as you can. Hold that position for a few seconds so that you know how a tightened fist feels. Then release it. Relax your hand and wiggle your fingers to loosen it even more. Next, tense the muscles in your forearm. Try to do this without tensing your hand again. You want to isolate each body part as you tense and relax it. Hold the tensed position long enough to register how it feels. Then release and shake it loose. Progress up the arm, tensing, holding, and releasing.

Move on to the other hand and arm, then to the shoulders and neck. Go on to your feet and move up your legs to the buttocks and lower back, always tensing, holding, and releasing. Do these exercises at least once a day, preferably at night, because they'll relax you and prepare you for sleep. Don't race through the exercises. Take your time. If you don't have the twenty or thirty minutes you need to do them all, spend five or ten minutes working on specific parts at a time.

Learn to control your breathing. In ordinary circumstances, most people breathe correctly, letting their abdomen expand and contract with each breath. This is called belly breathing. When stressed, however, people start panicking and tend to breathe more quickly and more shallowly. The chest rises and falls with each breath, indicating that the lungs are not expanding sufficiently to pull in oxygen and fully expel the carbon dioxide. One of the quickest ways to relax yourself is to slow your breathing. Concentrate on the rise and fall of your abdomen. Push out your stomach, not your chest, and take the time to empty your lungs fully. If you have a tendency to hyperventilate and slowing down your breathing isn't effective, hold your breath for as long as you can. Then resume breathing more slowly.

Problem-Solving: When you have a problem, it's best to figure out exactly what the problem is and what your options are. If you have a problem with someone else, you'll want to involve that person in formulating the options. Practicing assertive behavior, as discussed in chapter 6, will help you find a solution that satisfies you both.

In coming up with options, work to find at least three that could solve your problem. Call them Plan A, Plan B, and Plan C. That way, if you try an option and it doesn't work out, you have two other options. People who are prepared are less overwhelmed by stressful events. The key is to be flexible, so that if one plan doesn't work, you'll have no qualms about implementing the next plan.

Let's say you're afraid that you might have trouble handling the increased academic workload in college. Instead of worrying about what might happen, plan what you'll do in the event that you do have trouble with schoolwork. Plan A might be to talk with your instructors about your difficulties. Plan B might be to hire a tutor to help you. Plan C might be to drop one class and concentrate more on the other ones. When you know your options ahead of time, you're less likely to feel overwhelmed should problems develop.

2. Schedule "downtime" for yourself. You need relaxing time every day, not just once a week or when you've finished a major project. During your downtime, you don't do anything but relax or play. Watching television while you iron is not downtime because ironing is work. Listening to music or the sounds of nature can be relaxing if you're not also doing your homework. There's a time for homework (preferably a time when you're totally focused) and a time to relax. Downtime allows you to rest so that you do not accumulate stresses from day to day.

3. Reduce your caffeine intake. Caffeine is a stimulant.

It can make you feel jittery and irritable. It increases alertness, but it also sets your nerves on edge.

Reducing caffeine means reducing the amount of caffeinated coffee, tea, and soda you drink, the amount of chocolate you eat, and the number of medications you take that contain caffeine. You'd be surprised at all the items that contain caffeine, so make it a habit to check labels before buying a product.

Nicotine, found in cigarettes, is another stimulant you should avoid. Because smoking is addictive, it's a hard habit to give up, but one well worth the effort when working to reduce overall stress in your life.

4. Develop an exercise routine. This doesn't mean that you have to work out for hours each day. Simply taking a brisk walk for thirty minutes each day is enough to keep your body in good aerobic condition. Exercising also causes the brain to release endorphins, the body's own painkillers. In fact, scientists have discovered that the best measure for guarding against stress is regular exercise.

5. Create a calming environment around you. Play relaxing music, even if your preference is for rock or rap. You can listen to rock or rap when you want to be energized, but neither will do much to calm your nerves.

Create a "safe place" for yourself, especially if you live in an unsafe neighborhood. Everyone needs a place to go when they're stressed from the events of the day. If your home is not safe, find another place away from danger. Some people have found a special place in a park or in a corner of the library. Others have created a private spot in neighboring woods or by a creek.

Not only do you want a calm environment, you want

to surround yourself with calm people. Of course, this doesn't mean that you can't go to wild parties. However, you are defined in part by the people with whom you choose to spend the most time. If your friends are loud and abrasive, you are likely to feel more stressed. Level-headed, low-key people, on the other hand, seem more immune to stress.

6. Learn to stand up for yourself and express your feelings. This means saying no when you feel like saying no and setting appropriate limits with other people.

There are four main ways that a person can behave in relation to others. He can be aggressive, placing his own needs above anyone else's. He can be passive-aggressive, acting unintentionally in aggressive ways. He can be submissive, placing others' needs ahead of his own. Finally, he can be assertive, considering both his needs and the needs of others. An assertive person neither violates another person's space nor tolerates violation of his own space.

Imagine that you live next door to a man who doesn't own a lid for his garbage can. Every time he puts out his trash, either some of it blows into your yard or neighborhood dogs strew it all over your sidewalk. You're careful about covering your own trash so that it doesn't bother anyone else. How can you get your neighbor to act the same way?

If you adopt an aggressive stance, you may get up one morning, gather up all the trash in your yard, and dump it on your neighbor's lawn. Then you may tell him that either he gets a lid for his trash or you'll see to it that both yours and his end up on his front steps each week. You may look him in the eye, maybe shake your fist at him, and lean in close to be sure that he hears you correctly. Clearly, you are infringing on his space.

If you adopt a passive-aggressive stance, you will be too shy to confront your neighbor. But what if one day you forget to put your own trash can lid on? You will be genuinely surprised when interested dogs sniff your trash and overturn your can into your neighbor's yard. You won't see that you may be contributing to the problem.

If you adopt a submissive stance, you may pick up your neighbor's trash each and every time it blows into your yard. You won't complain, but you'll feel annoyed. If he notices what you're doing and comments on it, you'll simply shrug and say it's no big deal. That's what neighbors are for. Meanwhile you won't look him in the eye, you'll hang your head, and you may take a step back if he comes close. In other words, you'll let him walk all over you. The only way you'll know it really bothers you is that your stomach will probably feel like it is on fire.

If you adopt an assertive stance, you'll think about the problem before you confront your neighbor. You'll pick a time when he's not busy and ask to speak to him. Then you'll explain that his trash keeps blowing into your yard because there's no lid on his trash can. While you're talking, you'll look him in the eye and speak in a level tone of voice. You'll neither stand so close that he has to take a step back nor step back yourself if he advances. You will stand your ground.

If the neighbor seems perplexed about what to do, have some solutions ready. Suggest that he buy a cover and tie it to the garbage can so it won't fall off and blow away.

When people are assertive, they show respect both for

themselves and others. Sometimes you'll want to say no. If you relent and say yes, you'll feel angry at the person for putting you in that situation and at yourself for not having the guts to say what you really felt. Unresolved anger can lead to depression and, sometimes, aggressive acting out. When you say no and mean it, you show respect for yourself. You also stave off any anxious feelings about the situation and the people involved.

Setting limits goes along with saying no. People, especially family members, often push you to do more than you want to do. Or they give you unsolicited advice. Set limits by determining the boundaries of your relationship. When someone oversteps that boundary, recognize it and assert yourself. People don't have the right to run your life unless you give them that right.

7. Along with asserting yourself and setting limits, learn how to express anger appropriately. It's not enough just to recognize that you're angry, although that's a starting point. People explode and hurt others when they're angry, and that's just as inappropriate as holding in anger and ending up with a tension headache.

Learning to deal with your anger begins with recognizing when you're angry, with whom you're angry, and why you're angry. Once you realize that you're angry (the clenched teeth, the churning stomach, the tension headache), consider who can change that situation, and then clarify the situation that needs to be changed.

Sometimes you feel too angry to talk to the other person. When that happens, either try to calm yourself in order to gain perspective on the situation, or wear yourself out by exercising, cleaning, or playing a sport. The goal is to give yourself time to calm down and think more clearly. Taking your anger out by hitting things (even if they aren't the people) is not a good thing. It doesn't calm you down; most often it increases your anger.

It's okay to tell someone you're angry. Telling someone your feelings is far better than acting them out or holding them inside. But try to look beyond the anger to the feelings underneath. These feelings are often ones of hurt, shame, or envy. Be prepared for the other person to have a different interpretation of the situation. Listen if he presents it, because you might discover that your view of the situation was not entirely accurate. Then different solutions might present themselves.

Anger itself doesn't cause more stress. The way people react to anger is the problem. If you're honest with your feelings and present them assertively (not aggressively), you stand to reduce your stress, not make it worse.

If someone is angry with you, you can help him out and reduce your own stress by asking what has angered him and how he thinks the situation might be resolved.

8. Learn to manage your time better. Set priorities so that in a time crunch, you get the most important stuff done first. Set aside time to do schoolwork, time to be with friends, time to do chores or be at a job. And of course, give yourself some downtime so you won't be stressed by meeting everyone else's agenda.

Some people can accomplish more by keeping lists of things that need to be done. As they complete a task, they mark it off the list. This helps them realize how much they actually accomplish even if there are few outward signs.

Give yourself a time frame to accomplish certain things.

Some things need to be done right away; others can wait until tomorrow or the next day. If you try to accomplish too much in one day, you'll probably get frustrated and give up. Set short-term goals, and note when you've met them. Prioritize your tasks and do the important stuff first.

9. Get a pet if you can. Pets have been shown to decrease stress significantly. If you're allergic to animals or you can't have one where you live, consider getting fish. Goldfish are inexpensive and easy to maintain. Watching fish swim around in a tank is relaxing; that's why you see so many aquariums in doctors' offices.

10. Recognize that stress is more manageable at certain times than others. When you're overtired or ill, you're more likely to be overwhelmed by events that otherwise wouldn't seem so monumental. When you're not coping well, delay any decisions and distract yourself until you're better able to cope. When you're worried or tired, you won't make good decisions. Distract yourself from feeling anxious and unable to cope. Promise yourself that you'll deal with the situation when you're rested. Consider that on better days, this situation might not even seem like a problem. Then attend to your health and recovery. Chronically stressful situations (such as a loved one's illness) can affect your own health. So get plenty of rest yourself, and eat well.

When you accept that stress is an inevitable part of your life, you can find ways to contain it rather than run from it. Stress was never resolved by people's pretending that it didn't exist. As you become more adept at managing stress, you will find yourself more happy, more open to new experiences, and better able to get through the inevitable bumps in life.

The Origins of
Depression

When stressful situations are not managed successfully, people may react in self-defeating ways. As they start to isolate themselves and avoid the source of their fears, they become depressed as well as anxious.

Not surprisingly, depression and anxiety often go hand-in-hand. When people feel that they have no control over the events in their lives, they may become hopeless, negative, and despairing.

Donna

Donna was a shy teenager who used to avoid all social interactions—at least until she became friends with Sheila, a popular cheerleader. Sheila made it clear to her friends that Donna was to be included in all their activities, and because everyone liked Sheila, they accepted Donna as well. Donna never did overcome her discomfort in social situations, but she could tolerate the discomfort when Sheila was there with her. Sheila was her safety net.

The two girls were inseparable in high school. So when Sheila decided to go to an out-of-town college, Donna was devastated. How would she function without her friend? How could Sheila do this to her?

Donna argued and pleaded, but Sheila had her

heart set on that particular school. Seeing that Sheila wouldn't change her mind, Donna applied to the school, too, but was not accepted. What would she do?

All summer long Sheila prepared for college, and Donna worried what would happen to her at the local university. She felt that Sheila was deserting her, and she grew angry that nothing she did had any effect on her friend. She couldn't control events; her safety net would soon be gone.

The more hopeless Donna became, the more negative she grew. Without Sheila, she would never make any new friends. By summer's end, Donna was so anxious about going to college that she withdrew.

Perfectionist Parents

Living with perfectionistic, demanding parents is an enormous stress for many teenagers. If they try to meet the high expectations and fall short, their self-esteem suffers. Instead of blaming their parents for setting unrealistic goals, these teens blame themselves for not measuring up. Some keep trying to achieve; others give up. Those who continually fail become depressed. But it is a depression worsened by anxiety.

Hoping to one day meet their parents' expectations, kids study their parents constantly for signs of how to behave. This leads to physical stress from being alert all the time, and eventually to depression from not always succeeding in pleasing their parents.

Martin's parents were both perfectionistic and abusive. They had very rigid ideas of how children should behave.

Failure to meet their ideals resulted in beatings. Because Martin was the eldest, he felt responsible for his siblings' safety. He became good at tuning in to his parents' emotions, sensing when either one might fly off the handle.

By the time Martin graduated from high school, he suffered physical symptoms of anxiety: stomach problems and headaches. In addition, he had become very depressed because no matter how careful he was, he still could not control his parents' reactions.

Once Martin tried to reason with his parents. His father only hit him more. Another time Martin threatened to tell school officials. His father warned that the officials would tell the welfare people, who then would remove the kids from the home. "Then you'd all go to separate foster homes and never see each other again," he threatened.

Martin saw no end to the violence at home. In addition to being anxious, he grew despondent. "I will never be able to control my life," he told himself. This shows how helplessness (not being able to affect an outcome) leads to depression. If you can't do anything to change a situation for the better, you give up. Giving up leads to depression.

Combating depression and anxiety means successfully challenging cognitive distortions—mistaken beliefs that we have about certain events. Since stress is everywhere, the real cause of anxiety is what we tell ourselves about our ability to manage the stress. Look back at Martin's situation. He told himself that he would never be able to control events in his life. That was really a mistaken belief, and it contributed to his depression. Even though he was unable to stop his father's brutal beatings, that didn't mean that his life would always be out of control.

If you worry often about events in your life, stop and look at what you tell yourself when you worry. Making sweeping generalizations, especially negative ones, will only worsen the situation. Instead, make specific comments about the event at hand or your ability to manage the stress. Tell yourself, "Losing the race is unfortunate, but it's not the end of the world. I can always try again."

In fact, your ability to believe that usually you are in control relates to your success in life. Optimistic people always interpret events in their favor. Pessimistic people, on the other hand, blame themselves and put the worst possible spin on the event.

To reduce the likelihood of depression, it's important to build your self-esteem. You do that by staying involved in your world and being productive. People who have high self-esteem see themselves as effective. It's not necessarily that they are effective, only that they see themselves that way. Feeling is believing. That's where the self-talk comes in. What you say to yourself a hundred times a day is what you incorporate into your self-esteem.

For some people, however, practicing daily affirmations and striving toward short-term goals is not enough. If you are severely depressed, no amount of willpower can make you "come out of it." If you are unable to function independently (go to school, hold down a job, interact with friends) because of depression, you need to seek professional help. This is further discussed in chapter eleven.

Set small goals and work toward reaching them. As you see that you can meet these goals, you demonstrate effectiveness. That leads to increased self-esteem. If you set realistic goals, you won't become discouraged.

Part IV:
Treating Anxiety Disorders

Talk Therapy

When the field of psychoanalysis—or "talk therapy"—began, it was believed that anxiety stemmed from wanting to do something you know is not acceptable. This conflict originated in childhood. If a person was unable to face these unacceptable urges, he or she would divert the urges into specific phobias or feel compelled to perform certain behaviors over and over.

The process of psychoanalysis was developed to probe the origins of anxiety. Modern therapists may also try to connect a person's present conflict with some unresolved conflict in the past. The emphasis is on remembering the original conflict and talking it out. The problem is that often, knowing the source of the anxiety does not necessarily stop the behavior.

Defense mechanisms serve to keep us unaware of our anxiety. All defense mechanisms are unconscious; we're not aware of them at the time we use them. A therapist's job is to bring the use of these defense mechanisms to our awareness so that we understand the source of our anxiety. At that point, we can learn how to deal with the feelings of anxiety that the original source causes. The following are all different kinds of defense mechanisms.

↝ Repression: When you repress certain bad memories, you basically "forget" them. You don't do this intentionally; it just happens, usually when the memories are so horrible that they would cause great anxiety if they were remembered. Of course, repressed memories haven't disappeared. They are just removed from your awareness. But they still have enormous power to motivate you to behave in certain ways that you can't quite explain.

↝ Regression: A person resorts to regression when he feels overwhelmed by stress; he begins to behave in a way more suited to an earlier, less stressful time. For example, a four-year-old who gets a new baby sister may become stressed by all the attention his parents are giving the baby. As a result, he starts to act more babyish himself.

↝ Sublimation: When people have unacceptable impulses, they sometimes sublimate them by converting them into socially acceptable behaviors. For example, a sexually frustrated writer may go on to write erotic novels.

↝ Rationalization: If you've ever arrived in class without your homework and blamed it on your parents who sent you to bed early, you know what rationalization is. When you rationalize, you come up with a seemingly plausible explanation for your actions. The explanation will absolve you from blame, thereby alleviating any stress or anxiety about a situation.

↪ Displacement: Taking out your feelings on someone or something other than the cause of those feelings is called displacement. For example, you may get angry at your teacher about something and go home and yell at your sister. You tell yourself that you're mad at your sister for squeezing the toothpaste tube in the middle, but the truth is that she's done that lots of times and it never bothered you. Really you're angry with your teacher for assigning homework the night of your big game. But if you had complained about it, she would have given you even more work. Unable to let out your anger at your teacher, you displace it onto your unsuspecting sister.

↪ Projection: This occurs when someone disowns certain qualities that she doesn't like about herself and starts to attribute those qualities to other people. For example, a woman who can't accept that she is a gossip may unjustly accuse her neighbor of gossiping.

↪ Reaction Formation: This defense mechanism occurs when a person can't accept his own negative feelings but makes himself believe that his feelings are really the opposite. The young man who hates his father for beating him tells himself that he adores his father. When people say bad things about his father, the young man defends him. It's not a case of pretending to like his father; then his efforts would be conscious. He convinces himself that he really has such positive feelings.

The essence of traditional psychotherapy is to bring the original conflict to light, whether by examining defense mechanisms or by talking over your feelings. Since individuals manage their anxiety through unconscious means, it is the therapist's job to expose the means: the defense mechanisms. By gaining insight into the source of the anxiety, the individual supposedly will stop suffering.

However, psychotherapy alone is not always sufficient to overcome panic attacks and compulsive behavior. Doctors had to start considering other approaches to combating anxiety disorders, which I'll explain in the following chapters.

Cognitive and Behavioral Techniques

Cognitive and behavioral therapies involve more than just talking about anxiety and determining its root conflict. Cognitive therapists focus on changing your thinking, and behavioral therapists focus on changing your behavior. Many therapists incorporate both approaches in a holistic attempt to treat the disorder.

Physiological reasons may explain the beginnings of panic and phobias, but what you think—and what you do—about these conditions determines how well you are able to cope with them.

Self-Talk and Cognitive Distortions

As you have read, people worsen their anxiety with negative self-talk. Your heart skips a beat and you think, "Oh, no. I'm having a panic attack. I'd better get out of here before it gets worse." Your teacher assigns a speech in English class and immediately you start to feel sick. "I can't do this," you think. "I'll be too scared, and with everyone watching, I'll probably make a fool of myself." When you start telling yourself that you can't possibly handle a situation and that it will only get worse, your anxiety escalates.

Cognitive therapists would tell you to change your self-talk. Make it positive. Tell yourself you can handle the situation. If your heart skips a beat, tell yourself that this happens to everyone. If you have a panic attack, tell yourself that you can ride out the symptoms. A panic attack lasts only ten to twenty minutes at most, and you can tolerate discomfort that long. Learn to challenge your mistaken beliefs about your situation and your ability to handle it.

Here are some common cognitive distortions:

- ⌖ Overgeneralization: thinking that something bad that happened once will always happen under the same circumstances.

- ⌖ All or nothing thinking: thinking "I'm always out of control when I panic" instead of examining each panic episode separately to find out the cause.

- ⌖ Exaggeration: thinking "*Everyone* is looking at me."

- ⌖ Catastrophizing: predicting that the worst possible scenario is coming to pass; for example, thinking, "I'm going crazy" or "I'm dying" when you are having a panic attack. If you extend this line of thinking into the future, you will imagine many imminent disasters.

- ⌖ Underestimation: believing that you can't handle the situation without even trying. Common thoughts are, "I just don't know what to do when I'm anxious. I'm not strong enough to fight it."

Most of the time people make these statements to themselves without stopping to challenge the truth of them. If you want to reduce your anxiety, you must first learn to recognize your mistaken beliefs. Then you have to look for the fallacy in the belief and challenge it, substituting more supportive self-talk. Cognitive therapists understand that it is not so much the event that leads to anxiety as it is the way we feel about the event.

Making up and filling out a worksheet with the following headings can help you become more aware of your own mistaken beliefs. Whenever you feel anxious, jot down what's going on, using the list as a guide:

↪ The event

↪ Your thoughts about the event

↪ Cognitive distortion in that thinking

↪ Ways to challenge negative self-talk by substituting more supportive statements

The purpose of refraining from negative self-talk is to keep your anxiety from escalating. When something happens or you anticipate a scary event, your negative self-talk leads you to feel anxious. Once you look at the mistaken beliefs in your thinking and challenge them with more realistic, affirming statements, your anxiety should decrease. After all, it's not the event that makes you anxious; it's how you think about the event.

Let's say I've been invited out to dinner and I am starting to panic at the thought of eating in public (a realistic fear when I was a teenager). I would fill out the worksheet this way:

Event	Thoughts about the event	Cognitive distortion in that thinking	Positive self-talk
Invitation to dinner	I won't be able to swallow	I'm predicting the future	I'll be nervous. If I have trouble swallowing, I just won't eat.
	Everyone will be watching me eat.	Exaggeration: Surely not everyone will spend their time watching me.	Some people might notice me, but not everyone is going to be watching me eat.
	People will think something is wrong with me.	Predicting the future again.	My date might wonder why I'm not eating much, but no one else will care.
	I might die because I can't swallow.	Catastrophizing: I may feel as if I'm dying, but nobody dies from simply not swallowing.	I might gag for a second, but I won't die.

Dealing with Worrying

Sometimes it is not helpful to spend much time countering the negative self-talk. That's true if you obsessively worry. You might spend all day filling out worksheets on your fears. In those situations, it's probably better to try a different approach.

You can try time limiting—that is, indulging the urge to worry, but limiting it. First you set aside an hour (purposely choosing a long period of time) specifically in which to worry. Don't let your mind wander; keep returning to your worries.

At the end of the allotted time, stop worrying. If the thoughts come back, tell yourself you can't think about them until tomorrow.

Chances are you'll be bored before your time is up, and it will be hard to force the worrying after a while.

Another way to curb worrying is to visualize a big red stop sign every time a thought enters your head. If no one is around, shout "Stop" out loud at the same time. This behavior interrupts the thought. Although the thought may come back later, you can simply keep interrupting it. Soon enough, your mind learns to turn off that particular thought.

Techniques for Handling Panic

Before you can learn to tolerate the sensations of a panic attack or manage the anxiety associated with your phobic situation, you have to learn how to relax. Chapter six discusses how to practice progressive relaxation. If you practice it consistently, you will be aware when your muscles are tense and will know how to shake them loose.

When you breathe properly, your abdomen, not your chest, should rise and fall. Chest breathing is too shallow and is not conducive to relaxing. To make sure you are breathing correctly, lie on your back in a relaxed position. Place one hand on your belly and the other on your chest. Inhale slowly. The hand resting on your belly should rise more than the hand resting on your chest.

If that is not the case, practice exaggerating the movements as you inhale and exhale. Push your belly out as you inhale and deflate it when you exhale. Concentrate as much on exhaling as you do on inhaling. Not exhaling completely leads to a buildup of carbon dioxide and the inevitable feeling of panic.

When you are certain of your technique, stand up and continue to breathe, pushing out your abdomen. By exhaling completely, you will be forced to breathe more slowly and deeply. To ensure that you are breathing slowly at first, inhale to a silent count of 1–2–3. Hold that breath for two counts, then exhale just as slowly to another silent count of 3–2–1. Make sure to breathe through your nose. When you breathe through your mouth, you have a natural tendency to breathe more shallowly.

Now that you know how to relax and breathe properly, you can incorporate these techniques when you start to feel anxious. Imagine a ladder whose rungs represent how anxious you are. Mild anxiety is on the bottom rung, progressing up through moderate anxiety to panic at the top.

When you are in situations that make you feel anxious, visualize that ladder and where your anxiety fits. If you register only mild anxiety, stay as you are. If you register moderate anxiety, check your body for muscle tension. Relax your muscles and breathe more slowly.

If you find yourself hyperventilating (breathing quickly and in shallow breaths), you can do two things. Try to slow your breathing, which will be the opposite of what

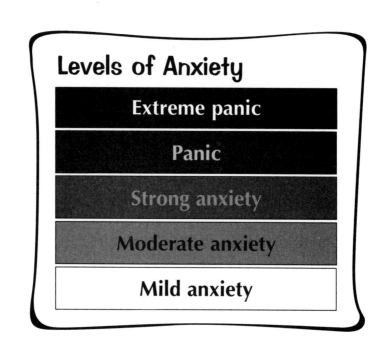

Levels of Anxiety

Extreme panic

Panic

Strong anxiety

Moderate anxiety

Mild anxiety

your body wants to do. Hold your breath as long as you can, then resume breathing more slowly. Concentrate on exhaling as much as inhaling. If all else fails, breathe into a paper bag (never a plastic bag). Breathing in air you have exhaled will adjust the level of carbon dioxide in your body, thus calming you down.

Techniques for Overcoming Phobias

Before anything else, you need to get accustomed to your internal sensations when you are distressed. You can learn to tolerate them. When you first notice that you are feeling anxious, pretend that you are a reporter and objectively note the sensations. For example, if your heart starts to beat faster, instead of giving in to your panic, simply notice the rapid beating. Note when your fingers start to feel tingly; wiggle them around and remind yourself that your fingers feel this way because an alarm has been triggered in your body and blood is being diverted from your fingertips to your larger muscles. Notice the butterflies in your stomach. Stay objective, reminding yourself that your stomach is reacting to the increased acidic juices.

It may help to write down on a separate sheet of paper all the physical sensations you have. If you are prone to negative self-talk, note what thoughts first come to mind when you sense distress. Challenge the distortions and continue to observe the sensations.

Event	Physical Sensations	Self–Talk

If at any point you feel yourself tensing up, concentrate on relaxing your muscles and breathing more slowly. Continue to observe the sensations as they peak and then subside. You can comment on the intensity of the feelings, but remain objective and do not react to the sensations. As they diminish, consider which feelings were the most difficult to tolerate. Why these feelings in particular? Did you associate them with something else? Feelings that you don't choose to fight often lose their control over you.

As you adjust to these uncomfortable sensations, keep using relaxation techniques whenever you catch yourself tensing up. Gradually you'll be able to tolerate more and more. Once you can tolerate your sensations, you're ready for the next step.

Since avoidance of a fearful situation only strengthens the phobia, a victim must face the dreaded situation in order to overcome his fear of it. There are two ways to accomplish this. One way is to create a hierarchy of stressful situations, much like the ladder used earlier. At the bottom, list the least stressful of the scenarios. The stress intensifies as you climb the ladder. This is called systematic desensitization. If this process is too overwhelming to do on your own, a therapist who specializes in desensitization and *in vivo* exposure (facing the phobia in person) can help you. Here's how it would be accomplished.

If a person were afraid of spiders, she might envision her hierarchy like this:

Spider Hierarchy
Holding a spider in my hand
Sitting next to a spider
Sitting next to a spider web
Stepping on a small spider
Hearing someone say that a spider ran into my closet
Hearing someone say there's a spider in the next room
Looking at a spider through a glass barrier in a zoo
Looking at a picture of a spider in a magazine

Clearly, just looking at a spider in a magazine is the least stressful scenario, so that is where she'll begin to desensitize herself to the fear. If she's a good visualizer, she probably starts to feel anxious. At that point, she observes the anxiety and relaxes her tense muscles. She takes several calming breaths until she can think about the picture without discomfort.

Then she moves to the next level, imagining herself looking at a live spider through a glass barrier at the zoo. As that picture stirs up anxiety, she is quick to relax her muscles and take calming breaths. If she is still anxious, she visualizes another scene that calms her. Some people visualize the ocean, watching the waves crash onto the beach while listening to the sounds of seagulls flying overhead. Whatever scenario represents a safe, calming place for you will work.

When the person is calm and relaxed from visualizing her safe place, she switches back to visualizing the spider. She stays with that scenario until she can visualize it without feeling anxious. On she goes up the ladder, visualizing, feeling anxious, and teaching herself to relax.

Obviously, this is a long process. It is not completed in one sitting or even in one day. By the time she can imagine holding a spider in her hand without feeling even a twinge of anxiety, she is ready to test herself by dealing with the real situation—in this case, a spider.

Sometimes it helps to keep a chart of your desensitizing sessions. Simply record what level of the ladder you are working on and how long it took you to master that level. If a particular level is not easy to master, record how much time you spent for each session on that level. Some people see more progress when their attempts are recorded on paper.

Exposure involves actually experiencing the anxiety provoking situations. The phobic person attempts this either with her therapist or another friend as a safe person. Otherwise, she may use medication to mask the symptoms of anxiety. If the person relies on a safe person or medication to get her through, she must give up the crutch as soon as possible and attempt it on her own. Most people who take medicine are surprised to discover that they relapse once they stop taking the medication.

Clearly, actual exposure is much more anxiety provoking than imagery exposure. It won't be as easy to calm yourself, so you must learn to retreat and recover. When the anxiety has lessened, you reexpose yourself to the situation and try to increase the time you spend in it. Even if you have to retreat twelve times, you still must reexpose yourself until you can deal with the situation.

When you can tolerate the least stressful situation on your ladder, you move on to the next one, always exposing, calming or retreating, and reexposing. The girl with the spider phobia would actually look at a spider in a magazine, not just imagine it. She'd go to the zoo, and she'd actually touch a spider. She'd do each of the things on her list until she had conquered her fear of spiders.

Handling Obsessions and Compulsions

Obsessive-compulsive disorder is best treated with medication, which is discussed in the next chapter. However, behavioral techniques can be used in addition to medication. The most successful techniques with obsessive-compulsive disorder are to delay responding to your urges and to distract yourself from the anxiety.

If you are a compulsive shopper, for example, you would tell yourself to wait until the next day to give in to the shopping urge. Compulsive checkers would tell themselves to wait an hour before getting up to check instead of trying to resist the urge entirely. The more you can delay, the more you get used to a little anxiety; just as you learned to tolerate discomfort in a panic attack, you can learn to tolerate the discomfort of ignoring a compulsion.

You try to stay objective and recount how you are feeling. Then you try to focus on something else.

You can monitor your success in delaying your urge to perform rituals or litanies by using a Magical Thinking Chart. Fill in each section, noting the unpleasant thought, the consequence of not performing your ritual or litany (in other words, what you think will happen if you don't perform the ritual), and your anxiety level (1–10, where 10 is extreme). Your goal is to gradually perform fewer rituals to reduce your anxiety. By using this chart, you can see your progress.

In addition, reality testing may help you learn to dismiss unpleasant thoughts without performing your rituals. For example, if your thought is:

Thought	Consequence of not performing compulsion	Anxiety level (1–10)	Reality Test	Compulsion Performed	Anxiety Level
I must turn the lock 5 times to make sure it's locked.	The door won't be locked, and robbers will break in.	10	Most people don't turn a lock 5 times.	I turned the lock 3 times.	7

Your goal is to use reality testing to talk yourself into performing fewer compulsions. As you reduce compulsive behavior, note your corresponding anxiety level. It will be high at first when you choose not to perform a ritual, but when the dire consequences you are expecting

77

don't actually happen, your anxiety level should go down. Eventually you will be able to ignore your need to perform your rituals.

Medications

Because of the physiological symptoms associated with anxiety, people seem to think that treating the symptoms will cure the disorder. Rarely does it work that way. Certain drugs will mask or temporarily treat an anxiety disorder, but they don't "cure" the anxiety. Most people need therapy to learn to manage anxiety disorders. Cognitive and behavioral therapists seem to offer the most hope because these types of therapies focus on actively changing a person's beliefs and behaviors.

Allowing for Setbacks

Some days you will be better able to manage your symptoms using these techniques. Other days you won't. When people have been subjected to more stress than usual (a prolonged illness or a loved one's illness) or are overtired, they may not be as successful in tolerating their symptoms or challenging their cognitive distortions. When you are having trouble, recognize it as only a temporary setback. Under other circumstances, you would be more on top of your situation. Always keep your self-talk positive.

Using Medication

Anxiety disorders typically cause predictable symptoms: a rapidly beating heart, a nervous stomach, tense muscles, and blushing. Wouldn't it make sense, then, to take medications that repress these particular signs of anxiety?

Not necessarily. In addition to all the other causes of anxiety, a person can feel anxious because of certain medical conditions or because he or she has taken prescription or street drugs. If the actual cause is not addressed, the symptoms of anxiety are not easily managed. Thus your first plan of attack in treating anxiety should be to see a doctor who can rule out any contributing medical problems. Be sure to tell your doctor about all the medicines you've been taking, including any illegal drugs. Certain drugs can induce panic attacks, and your doctor needs to know all the facts.

Obviously, if a medical condition is causing the symptoms, that has to be treated first. Often the anxiety disappears as the medical condition is treated. If medications or drugs are causing the symptoms, they have to be changed or stopped altogether. Then, depending on the anxiety disorder, medication may be considered.

Years ago when I had so much trouble swallowing, my parents took me to the doctor. He initially suspected swollen tonsils, but after a complete workup, he found no physical cause. "You're having panic attacks," he said.

"Well, is there something I can take for it?" I asked.

He thought a moment and then scribbled something on a prescription pad. "Have your parents get this filled," he said. "It should help."

I never knew what he prescribed, but I gave the form to my parents and sat at home waiting for my relief. I had high expectations. I was going to be normal from now on when I had to eat in public. All I had to do was take this medicine (I hoped it was liquid, because I couldn't swallow pills), and I'd be calm and collected.

The only problem was that it didn't quite work that way. I took the medicine twice a day, and I gradually had less difficulty swallowing, but I didn't see the instant relief I expected. I still got nervous when I had to stand up in front of a class, and I still got a sick feeling before every major test I took. It was disappointing to discover that the medicine didn't take away my anxiety completely.

Many people think that there is a magic pill out there. Medication will help relieve your symptoms, but as discussed in previous chapters, there is no single "cure."

Types of Medication

There are five basic types of medication used to treat anxiety disorders. The first group is the antidepressants, including the tricyclic antidepressants (called TCAs) and the MAO inhibitors (also known as MAOIs). Both of these types of medications affect two neurotransmitters in the brain, norepinephrine and serotonin. MAO is a chemical in the brain that breaks down the norepinephrine and serotonin circulating in the brain. An MAO inhibitor prevents this chemical from breaking down and reabsorbing these two neurotransmitters.

Another group of antidepressants is the selective serotonin reuptake inhibitors (SSRIs). These medications specifically target the neurotransmitter serotonin and keep the neurons from reabsorbing it too quickly.

A third type of medication used is the benzodiazepines, the minor tranquilizers and the more sedating drugs. This is the group most often preferred (and abused) by people, because the relief is the quickest.

A fourth type of medication is the beta-blockers. These drugs are often used to treat high blood pressure and manage the symptoms associated with anxiety: pounding heart, blushing, and sweating.

The fifth type of medication used is the antihistamines, which correct inner ear disturbances that may produce anxiety symptoms.

Your doctor will determine when medication is appropriate and which type would work best to handle your symptoms. In any case, a combination of medication and cognitive/behavioral therapy provides the most lasting relief from anxiety.

Treating Panic Disorder

Panic disorder, during which panic attacks arise seemingly out of the blue, responds best to low doses of the TCAs. These medications, including imipramine (Tofranil), desipramine (Norpramin), amitriptyline (Elavil), and trazodone (Desyrel) are all effective in curbing panic attacks, although they do not affect the anticipatory anxiety that often accompanies panic disorder.

TCAs target the locus ceruleus, the part of the brain that actually causes panic attacks. TCAs actually prevent panic attacks from occurring, so medication should be considered first in treating this disorder.

People who use TCAs also need to practice cognitive and behavioral techniques to reduce their anticipatory anxiety. That involves challenging this cognitive distortion (I'm so nervous that I'm going to have a panic attack!) and practicing positive self-talk and relaxation techniques. Once they learn that their panic attacks are under control, they won't have to live in fear that the attacks will resurface in uncomfortable situations.

TCAs are not addictive; people need not worry about long-term use of these medications. Unfortunately, TCAs have some unpleasant side effects, such as dry mouth, and they can take up to four weeks to begin working.

If a person is unable to find relief using TCAs, a doctor might prescribe an MAOI. MAOIs often work quite well, but they can lead to a dangerous rise in blood pressure if the person eats cheese or certain meats, or drinks wine. In fact, when taking MAOIs, you must follow a very strict diet and avoid nasal decongestants and other medications that don't combine well with MAOIs. Phenelzine (Nardil) is the most commonly prescribed MAOI. Warnings about drug interactions are always included on packages, but you should ask your doctor or pharmacist for more information, especially if you have questions.

When people object to the side effects of TCAs and the dietary requirements of MAOIs, a doctor might try an SSRI instead. These newer antidepressants have fewer side effects, although in some people they may cause agitation. No one really understands why antidepressants block panic attacks, but they do. If anxiety is complicated by depression, a doctor might prescribe a higher dosage of these antidepressants, as panic disorder responds to low doses.

The benzodiazepines are used to manage the signs of anticipatory anxiety, but they are ineffective in preventing panic attacks. Alprazolam (Xanax) is commonly prescribed these days on a short-term basis. It provides rapid relief (within twenty minutes) that lasts approximately four hours. Combined with TCAs, benzodiazepines can be entirely effective in controlling panic and anticipatory anxiety. The drawback is that benzodiazepines are highly addictive.

Simple Phobias

When people are afraid of animals, snakes, heights, or water, imipramine can be used to manage the panic attacks that accompany the phobias. However, it does nothing about the avoidance behavior that maintains the fears. Some people require benzodiazepines in order to practice the behavioral techniques used to desensitize phobics. The short-acting benzodiazepines bring quick relief and a blunting of feelings (meaning that you won't sense your distress as acutely), which allows many people to confront the situations they fear. However, the use of benzodiazepines has to be a temporary measure and a prelude to desensitizing yourself without medication. Obviously, you don't prescribe these medications for yourself. If your doctor thinks benzodiazepines are necessary to help you deal with your fears, he or she will prescribe them for you.

If a doctor determines that your phobia is a result of an inner ear dysfunction, he or she will probably prescribe antihistamines and decongestants, such as Antivert and Sudafed. However, don't try self-medicating just because some of these medications are available over the counter. Only a doctor trained in recognizing and treating inner ear dysfunction should prescribe medicine for this disorder.

People who are afraid of public exposure or humiliation often benefit from beta blockers. These medications (specifically propranolol, or Inderal, and clonidine, or Catapres) control the manifestations of anxiety: the pounding heart, the blushing cheeks, the sweaty brow. Many people are able to handle potentially scary public encounters only when they take medication first. Without the physical signs of distress to react to, they do not develop further symptoms. The medications called SSRIs are often useful in treating social phobias, but they target panic and depressive symptoms, not generalized anxiety. A combination of beta blockers or benzodiazepines and SSRIs is usually more successful.

Obsessive-Compulsive Disorder

With this disorder, medication is the first line of defense. The antidepressant clomipramine (Anafranil) is the treatment of choice and has been used for years in Europe. However, it has some unpleasant side effects, including weight gain, so many doctors prefer to prescribe the SSRIs. The antidepressants that target serotonin seem to have the best potential for disrupting the compulsive behavior and obsessive thoughts of this disorder. Fluoxetine (Prozac), sertraline (Zoloft), paroxetine (Paxil), and more recently Luvox are all important in controlling this disorder.

Sometimes medication alone does not control all the symptoms, and behavioral strategies are needed to supplement the medicine. Delaying and distracting techniques are helpful in providing some measure of control over this disorder, but in general, medication works best. Whatever the specific cause of obsessive-compulsive disorder, it appears to be at least partially chemical in nature.

Generalized Anxiety

Although there are drawbacks to using benzodiazepines, some people simply have too much anxiety to learn to use behavioral techniques without first calming their nerves with benzodiazepines. The TCAs and MAOIs are not helpful with generalized anxiety because they specifically work to prevent panic attacks.

Benzodiazepines are prescribed for short-term or sporadic use. When a person has become dependent on them, he or she will have to taper the dose very slowly under a doctor's supervision to come off of them.

Problems with Using Medication

Medications provide quick and occasionally lasting relief, but there are drawbacks to reliance on them. As mentioned earlier, medications, especially benzodiazepines, are not particularly helpful in overcoming phobias.

Using drugs to address your anxiety teaches you to rely on something other than yourself. I had to learn to control my physical symptoms of anxiety when I ate in public. If my doctor had found a magic pill, I never would have realized that I could manage the anxiety by using cognitive and behavioral techniques. While medications are useful in treating chemical disturbances, they are short-term solutions for uncomfortable feelings. This becomes a problem when people rely on the medication rather than their own ability to talk themselves out of their anxiety. This ability is best developed by practicing stress-reducing cognitive and behavioral strategies.

Getting Professional Help

At what point should you consider getting professional help? The answer isn't clear-cut. Some people can tolerate more anxiety than others before they feel compelled to do something about it. Some people don't mind seeking professional help; others believe that they should be strong enough to handle their problems themselves. The bottom line is this: When anxiety interferes with your life so much that you are not able to carry on your normal activities on a daily basis, you need professional help.

People who break a leg or have appendicitis have no qualms about going to a doctor. Why should mental anguish be any different? You wouldn't expect a person to be strong enough to heal a broken leg on his own, would you? But people often think that a person should be able to manage his anxiety without help.

If you suffer disabling panic attacks or obsessions or are unable to overcome your phobias, you need professional help. This doesn't always mean a psychiatrist. Since anxiety disorders can be the result of chemical changes in your brain or medical conditions, it makes sense to have your primary-care physician check you out before thinking that the trouble is "all in your head."

In addition, many communities are now observing Anxiety Screening Day. Various mental health agencies and counseling offices conduct free assessments for people who believe they suffer from anxiety. Unfortunately, some mental health practitioners assume that if you seek treatment, you probably have a psychological disorder. The truth is that people can demonstrate anxiety symptoms without having a psychological problem. For that reason, most people could benefit from seeing their primary-care doctor first. If nothing physical shows up to account for your anxiety, then you should look for psychological explanations.

Primary-Care Doctors

Your primary-care doctor—your regular family doctor who generalizes in medicine—will do a workup to determine possible physical causes of your anxiety. That may entail blood work, X rays, and a thorough physical exam. She will probably ask about your family history as well, so know ahead of time if any aunts, uncles, grandparents, or siblings have certain psychological disorders. If the doctor rules out physical problems, she may refer you to a mental health professional for treatment.

Finding a Therapist

There are several important factors to consider if you are thinking about seeing a therapist. If you have medical insurance, you will want to find someone who is covered by your plan. In addition, you will want to see someone with whom you feel compatible and who you know is competent. So how do you go about finding the right therapist?

First of all, if you or your parents have insurance to pay for mental health treatment, you need to find out which therapists are covered. Some insurance groups have specific contracts with individuals or agencies to provide services, and those people will be your only choices. If you have no insurance and a limited ability to pay, you will probably have to go to a community mental health center. Mental health centers charge people based on their ability to pay. They use a sliding-scale fee to determine how much, if anything, services will cost.

Finding a therapist with whom you will work well is more difficult to do ahead of time. Word of mouth is nice, but the therapist your friend uses may not be to your liking. Also, seeing the therapist that your friend uses could lead to uncomfortable situations. What if you and your friend have a falling out? Will your therapist remain impartial? Therapists have different personalities and approaches, and you can't tell what the person will be like until you actually meet with him or her.

The only way to be satisfied with a therapist is to assess how you feel around him or her. If you are still uncomfortable after five or six sessions, you might discuss finding someone else. Bear in mind, however, that therapy itself is not a pleasant and anxiety-free process. After all, you are trying to learn some techniques that take time and effort to acquire. You are also taking a look at some problems—traumatic events or situations—that will undoubtedly stir up uncomfortable feelings.

Above all, you want to find a therapist who is competent, well-trained, and responsible. Many insurance companies require you to see someone who is licensed, which means that he or she has passed a national exam and had a certain number of years of education and supervision.

Additionally, you need to find someone who understands all the treatments available for anxiety disorders, including the cognitive and behavioral components as well as the appropriate medication for your particular disorder. Some people who specialize in treating anxiety advertise themselves that way; others are simply knowledgeable in the area from past experience.

Types of Therapists

When choosing a therapist, you should consider psychiatrists, psychologists, clinical social workers, licensed professional counselors or outpatient therapists (the usual designation at a mental health center), and clinical nurses.

Psychiatrists are the only ones who are also medical doctors. They are therefore the only ones who can prescribe medication. However, a visit to a psychiatrist's office is costly (usually more than $100 per thirty-minute visit) and some are only comfortable discussing and prescribing medication. If an undiagnosed medical condition is clouding the picture, the psychiatrist might be quicker at spotting it, but you do not necessarily have to see a psychiatrist to get quality care. Often psychologists and social workers refer their clients who need medication to psychiatrists with whom they have a working relationship.

Psychologists have a Ph.D. or a Psy.D. degree. They are not medical doctors, but have undergone a course of study for several years and have had experience in a clinical setting. They are often knowledgeable about testing and can both administer and assess psychological tests if any are needed to diagnose your disorder.

Clinical social workers may have either an M.S.W.

degree or a doctorate in social work. They are usually very well trained, providing most of the services to clients in mental health settings. They are also slightly less costly than psychologists and definitely less expensive than psychiatrists. Their sessions usually run about $80 an hour.

Psychiatric nurses, or clinical nurses, are also good choices because of their familiarity with medications and physical disorders. They are registered nurses with advanced degrees (usually a master's degree) in counseling.

Is one category better than another? Not necessarily. It really comes down to the individual's level of competence and personality. Just because your insurance policy requires that you see a psychologist, for example, doesn't mean that clinical social workers or clinical nurses are not as competent. Also, some companies prefer social workers over psychologists because they charge less for services.

Ethical Behavior

No matter what the profession, all therapists are bound by the same set of ethics. They are not allowed to have a physical relationship with you (even if you would be receptive to one) and are not allowed to threaten or coerce you. If that ever happens, you have the right to stop services immediately and report the therapist to the licensing board. If you are afraid to report the therapist yourself, tell your story to another reputable therapist.

Likewise, therapists should not spend your time discussing their own problems (unless there is a connection) or asking you to do them favors. Therapy is a business relationship. The therapist provides the services, and you pay for them. Becoming friends with your therapist so that you can do things together alters that business relationship, as well as being unethical.

Length of Treatment

How long will you be in treatment? Insurance companies often specify how many sessions they will pay for, based on the diagnosis. Beyond that, your therapist will recommend that you stay in treatment as long as it takes to gain mastery over your disorder. Some people function well seeing the doctor once every three months for medication. Others need to see their therapist more often to practice behavioral techniques to manage their anxiety. It is no longer a requirement that a person see a therapist every week in order to make life changes. When you can handle your anxiety without professional help, you are done with treatment. That is not necessarily left up to the therapist to decide.

Support Groups

Support groups are particularly helpful for people with anxiety disorders. Participants learn how others with anxiety have managed their disorders, and because the setting is public, they learn how to improve their social skills at the same time. Support groups may or may not be run by professionals. Sometimes former clients start a group to get together with others like themselves. They share advice on what strategies have worked for them and which therapists were most helpful. Most of these groups are not closed, meaning that people can join and drop out as they choose. It's helpful to have a professional therapist guide you in your recovery, but there's a lot to be said for having allies who share your symptoms.

Trauma—Recognizing the Steps to Healing

If you have been severely traumatized, you need professional help. Simply escaping the traumatic situation is not enough, because the memory of the trauma remains to haunt you and can create lasting feelings of anxiety or panic. Healing happens as you master three steps. First, you have to remember what happened and reexperience the impact. For most people, that does not feel safe, which is why they need to do their remembering with a therapist.

The second step is dealing with those feelings and grieving for your losses. The most prevalent feelings that surface in sexual abuse survivors are shame and guilt. These feelings are harder to accept than hurt and anger because they mean that people feel responsible for being abused. Therapy is helpful in dispelling the idea that the victim had any control over his or her situation. Of course, accepting how powerless you once were is a scary proposition. The feeling stage of treatment lasts a long time.

The final step is to move on and know how to protect yourself in the future. Whatever it takes to create a feeling of safety is what the survivor and therapist address. Working through these issues is a long process, but it is necessary for achieving peace.

Hospitalization

Sometimes anxiety is so disabling that it requires hospitalization. Inpatient treatment is considered only when a person is thought to be a danger to himself or others, or is unable to meet his everyday needs. Some people become suicidal when they panic. They fear that no one ever will be able to help them, so they try to take their own lives. If you have these feelings, you will need to stay in a hospital where staff can keep you safe until your panic has been treated.

Sometimes people are hospitalized so that they can undergo more extensive testing. When physical disorders are suspected as the cause of anxiety, patients may be hospitalized while the physical cause is being diagnosed.

When people can no longer attend to their everyday needs—such as going to work, buying groceries, and taking care of their families—because of extreme anxiety, they may need to be hospitalized either in the psychiatric wing of a general hospital or in a psychiatric hospital. Hospitalization is always a last resort, and the stays are as short as possible. For many anxiety sufferers, hospitalization comes as a relief. Hospital staff involve the patient's family as much as possible, with the goal of sending the patient home at the first possible opportunity.

Needing professional help is not a crime, nor is it something to be ashamed of. Anxiety disorders are complicated problems. Some people can learn all they need to know about managing anxiety by reading various books like this one. Others need to talk with therapists to learn how to practice the strategies correctly. However you deal with your anxiety is the "right" way as long as it helps you to gain control over your symptoms. There is no reason to let anxiety take over your life. There are many groups, organizations, and professionals that can help you. You owe it to yourself to seek support and advice.

Appendix:
Medications Used in Treating Anxiety Disorders

Generic Name	Brand Name	Generic Name	Brand Name
Antidepressants		**Benzodiazepines**	
(TCAs and MAOIs)		alprazolam	Xanax
amitriptyline	Elavil	chlordiazepoxide	Librium
clomipramine	Anafranil	clonazepam	Klonopin
desipramine	Norpramin	diazepam	Valium
doxepin	Sinequan	lorazepam	Ativan
imipramine	Tofranil	temazepam	Restoril
nortriptyline	Pamelor	triazolam	Halcion
trazodone	Desyrel		
phenelzine	Nardil	**Other Medications**	
tranylcypromine	Parnate	(beta-blockers and antihistamines)	
		Antivert	
		Marezine	
Antidepressants (SSRIs)		Dramamine	
fluoxetine	Prozac	Benadryl	
sertraline	Zoloft	Atarax	
paroxetine	Paxil	Ritalin	
fluvoxamine	Luvox	Dexedrine	
venlafaxine	Effexor	Sudafed	
citalopram	Celexa	Dimetapp	
nefazodone	Serzone		

Glossary

adrenaline   Hormone secreted by the adrenal glands that raises the blood pressure, causing the heart to pound and the senses to become alerted to the possibility of danger.

aggressive   Disposed to dominate without regard for the feelings of others.

agoraphobia   Extreme, irrational fear of being in open or public places.

"all or nothing" thinking   Tendency to assume the worst in a situation without first examining the reality.

anticipatory anxiety   Tendency to make a situation worse by imagining a negative outcome in advance.

antidepressant   Class of medication designed to reduce mental depression.

antihistamine   Medication used to reduce allergic reactions.

assertiveness   Acting with confidence without infringing on the rights of others.

behavioral reaction   The actions a person takes in response to another person's actions.

benzodiazepines   Group of drugs, including tranquilizers; often prescribed to alleviate panic attacks.

beta-blocker   Medication used to relieve high blood pressure and the symptoms of anxiety disorders.

bruxism   Grinding of the teeth, especially during stress.

catastrophize   To predict disaster when having a panic attack.

cognitive distortion Mistaken beliefs about events that cause stress; conviction that the worst will occur as a result.

cognitive reaction Way of thinking about anxiety that may actually increase the severity of anxiety.

defense mechanism Unconscious mental approach to a problem to try to resolve it.

displacement Transfer of anger against a powerful person to another person who poses no threat.

downtime Period specifically set aside for relaxation, without the need for accomplishing any task.

exposure Act of putting oneself in actual contact with the object of a phobia.

hypochondriac Person who frequently complains about various, often imaginary, physical ailments.

insomnia Inability to fall asleep or stay asleep; may have a physical or psychological basis.

irritable bowel syndrome Disorder of the colon involving alternate diarrhea and constipation;worsened by anxiety.

mitral valve prolapse Nondangerous heart condition that causes a backflow of blood; the accompanying pounding of the heart may cause anxiety and thus lead to a panic attack.

obsessive-compulsive disorder Mental disorder involving the need to repeat a behavior, such as handwashing.

overgeneralize To believe that a stressful event will always occur under the same conditions.

passive-aggressive Unconsciously disposed to act in a demanding way, without regard for the feelings of others.

phobia Long-lasting and irrationally strong fear of an object or a situation. Simple phobia is fear of a specific thing; social phobia refers to the fear of embarrassing oneself in public.

physiological Pertaining to physical symptoms of the body.

rationalization Application of plausible and credible motives to questionable behavior.

reaction formation Defense mechanism by which one credits oneself with good motives when they are actually negative.

regression Defense mechanism in which one reverts to an earlier, less stressful, period of life.

repression Defense mechanism in which one unconsciously "forgets" traumatic events.

stimulant Substance that causes a temporary increase of the function of the body or parts of the body.

sublimation Defense mechanism in which one disguises unacceptable impulses by changing them into socially acceptable behaviors.

submissive Having a tendency to give in to others, putting their concerns ahead of your own.

systematic desensitization Gradual elimination of fears by coming into repeated contact with the feared object.

Tourette's syndrome Condition in which a person has an uncontrollable urge to scream, shout, and use obscene language.

Ulcer Open sore in the stomach wall caused by excess production of stomach acids, sometimes as a result of stressful conditions.

Where to Go for Help

Hotlines

Anxiety/Panic
(800) 647–2642

Depression
(800) 969–6642
(800) 243–2525

Emotions Anonymous
(612) 647–9712

National Foundation for Depressive Illness
(800) 248–4344

National Mental Health
(800) 468–1515 (twenty-four hours a day, seven days a week))

Youth Crisis Hotline
(800) 448–4663

Organizations

Anxiety Disorders Association of America
11900 Parklawn Drive, Suite 100
Rockville, MD. 20852-2624
(301) 231-9350
Web site: http://www.adaa.org

Freedom From Fear
308 Seaview Avenue
Staten Island, NY 10305
(718) 351-1717
E-mail: fffnadsd@aol.com

National Alliance for the Mentally Ill (NAMI)
200 North Glebe Road, Suite 1015
Arlington, VA. 22203-3754
(800) 950-NAMI
Web site: http://www.nami.org

National Anxiety Foundation
3135 Custer Drive
Lexington, KY 40517–4001

National Mental Health Association
1021 Prince Street
Alexandria, VA 22314-2971
(800) 969-NMHA
Web site: http://www.nmha.org

Obsessive Compulsive Foundation
P.O. Box 70
Milford, CT 06460
(203) 878–5669

Phobics Anonymous
P.O. Box 1180
Palm Springs, CA 92263
(619) 322–COPE

Web Sites

Anxiety Disorders
http://www.nimh.nih.gov/publicat.anxiety.htm

Noodles' Panic-Anxiety Page
http:www.algy.com/anxiety/panic.html

For Further Reading

Babior, Shirley and Carol Goldman. *Overcoming Panic, Anxiety and Phobias.* Duluth, MN: Whole Person Associates, 1996.

Benson, Herbert, and Eileen Stuart. *The Wellness Book.* New York: Simon & Schuster, 1992.

Berent, Jonathan. *Beyond Shyness.* New York: Simon & Schuster, 1993.

Bilodeau, Lorraine. *The Anger Workbook.* Center City, MN: Hazelden Educational Materials, 1992.

Bourne, Edmund. *The Anxiety and Phobia Workbook.* Oakland, CA: New Harbinger Publications, Inc., 1995.

Carlton, Jean. *Panic No More.* Tulsa, OK: Stonehorse Press, 1994.

Carter, Les, and Frank Minirth. *The Anger Workbook.* Nashville, TN: Thomas Nelson, 1993.

Davis, Martha, Elizabeth Robbins Eshelman, and Matthew McKay. *The Relaxation and Stress Reduction Workbook.* Oakland, CA: New Harbinger Publications, 1995.

Dumont, Raeann. *The Sky is Falling.* New York: W.W. Norton and Co., 1997.

Feniger, Mani. *Journey From Anxiety to Freedom.* Rocklin, CA: Prima Publishing, 1997.

Lark, Susan. *Anxiety and Stress*. Berkeley, CA: Celestial Arts, 1996.

Markway, Barbara, Cheryl Carmin, C. Alex Pollard, and Teresa Flynn. *Dying of Embarrassment*. Oakland, CA: New Harbinger Publications, 1998.

McKay, Matthew, Martha Davis, and Patrick Fanning. *Thoughts and Feelings*. Oakland, CA: New Harbinger Publications, 1997.

Peurifoy, Reneau. *Overcoming Anxiety*. New York: Henry Holt and Co., 1997.

Potter, Dr. Beverly. *The Worrywart's Companion*. Berkeley, CA: Wildcat Canyon Press, 1997.

Sapolsky, Robert. *Why Zebras Don't Get Ulcers*. New York: W.H. Freeman and Co., 1998.

Schwartz, Jeffrey M., with Beverly Beyette. *Brain Lock*. New York: Regan Books, 1996.

Simpson, Carolyn, and Dwain Simpson. *Coping With Post-Traumatic Stress Disorder*. New York: Rosen Publishing Group, 1997.

Zuercher-White, Elke. *An End to Panic*. Oakland, CA: New Harbinger Publications, 1995.

Index